SNACK AND SANDWICH
C·O·O·K·B·O·O·K

GOLDEN APPLE PUBLISHERS

SNACK AND SANDWICHES COOKBOOK

A GOLDEN APPLE PUBLICATION/
PUBLISHED BY ARRANGEMENT WITH OTTENHEIMER PUBLISHERS INC.

JUNE 1986

GOLDEN APPLE IS A TRADEMARK OF GOLDEN APPLE PUBLISHERS

ALL RIGHTS RESERVED
COPYRIGHT © 1986 BY OTTENHEIMER PUBLISHERS, INC.

THIS BOOK MAY NOT BE REPRODUCED IN WHOLE OR IN PART,
BY MIMEOGRAPH OR ANY OTHER MEANS WITHOUT PERMISSION.
For Information Address: GOLDEN APPLE PUBLISHERS,
666 FIFTH AVENUE, NEW YORK, N.Y. 10103

ISBN 0-553-19855-6

Contents

Party Snacks	5
Sweet Snacks	25
Breads	38
Light Meals	47
Sandwiches	57
Equivalent Measures	94
Index	95

Party Snacks

Anchovy Sandwiches

- ½ loaf day-old homestyle bread, unsliced
- 10 anchovy fillets
- 4 tablespoons softened butter
- 2 tablespoons prepared mustard
- 4 hard-cooked eggs, finely chopped
- ¼ cup chopped dill or ¼ cup dill, parsley, and chives combined
- Dash of freshly ground black pepper
- Vegetable oil combined with butter for frying (about 2 tablespoons of each)

Trim crusts from bread and slice it into 12 thin slices about 1/8 inch thick. In a small bowl, chop anchovies and mash them together with butter, mustard, finely chopped eggs, herbs, and pepper. Spread this smooth mixture on 6 slices of the bread. Top each slice with its covering piece of bread. Refrigerate them for up to 3 days.

When ready to serve, melt combined oil and butter in a 12-inch skillet. Fry sandwiches, 2 or 3 at a time, until they are golden brown. Drain sandwiches, cut in quarters, and serve them hot. Makes 24 hors d'oeuvres.

Grilled Appetizer Sandwiches

8 slices sandwich bread　　　　　**Melted butter**
Dijon mustard
1 (6-ounce) package Emmenthal or Swiss cheese, sliced

Cut bread into 24 fancy shapes, using small, wet cutters. Spread with mustard. Cut cheese slices into fancy shapes matching the bread. Assemble into 12 sandwiches, using 2 pieces of cheese in each sandwich.

Grease a hot griddle or large heavy skillet with fresh pork fat or melted butter. Place sandwiches on griddle, then brush tops with melted butter.

Grill sandwiches until browned, then turn to brown other side.

Arrange cheese trimmings on top of each sandwich and drizzle or brush with additional butter. Remove from heat and slide griddle under broiler. Broil for several minutes or until cheese is bubbly. Makes 12 sandwiches.

Bugs On a Log

1 bunch celery　　　　　　　　**1 (14- to 15-ounce) box**
1 cup peanut butter　　　　　　**raisins**

Clean celery and slice into 2-inch pieces. Fill celery with peanut butter. Dot peanut butter with raisins to create "bugs on a log." Makes about 20 snacks.

Herb-Crusted Cauliflower

½ cauliflower　　　　　　　　　**Salt and pepper**
2 cups fresh bread crumbs　　　**2 eggs**
½ teaspoon mixed herbs　　　　**4 tablespoons milk**
¼ teaspoon oregano　　　　　　**Oil for deep frying**
¼ cup grated cheese

Trim cauliflower; remove outer green leaves and core. Cut into flowerettes. Drop flowerettes into boiling salted water; return water to boil and boil 2 minutes. Drain, cool.

When cold, dip into combined beaten eggs and milk; then roll in combined bread crumbs, herbs, oregano, cheese, salt, and pepper. Deep-fry in hot oil, a few at a time, so oil stays hot. Fry until golden brown. Drain on paper towels. Makes 4 to 6 servings.

Herb-Crusted Cauliflower

Garlic-Butter Chips

Fried Cheese

3 tablespoons butter	½ pound Kasseri cheese, sliced ½ inch thick
1 egg, well beaten	
1 teaspoon flour	3 tablespoons brandy
	Juice of ½ lemon

Heat butter in a large frying pan until melted and the foam has subsided. Beat egg and flour together. Dip cheese slices in egg mixture and fry until well browned on both sides.

Gently warm brandy; ignite it and pour it over cheese in skillet. Squeeze lemon juice over cheese and serve with crusty bread and sauce from pan. Makes 4 servings.

Cheese Ball

2 (3-ounce) packages cream cheese	½ teaspoon grated onion or onion juice
1 (5-ounce) jar sharp Cheddar cheese spread	½ teaspoon Worcestershire sauce
1 (5-ounce) jar Roquefort cheese spread	¼ cup undiluted evaporated milk
1 (5-ounce) jar Smoky cheese spread	½ cup walnuts, finely chopped

Let the 4 cheeses stand at room temperature for an hour or so. Put them in a mixing bowl with onion and Worcestershire. Mix with a fork until smooth and well blended. Stir in milk, a little at a time, and then cover and chill until firm. This will take about 4 hours or overnight.

Shape cheeses into a ball; roll in chopped nuts. Chill until ready to serve. Serve on a large platter with a parsley or watercress garnish and crisp crackers or wafers. Makes about 8 servings.

Cheese and Herb Spread

1 (6-ounce) cream cheese, at room temperature	2 tablespoons fresh mint, chopped
1 cup Feta cheese, finely crumbled	Salt to taste
½ cup unflavored yogurt	1 small clove garlic, crushed
2 tablespoons chives, finely chopped	Tomato slices
2 tablespoons fresh dill, chopped	Cucumber slices
	Black olives
	Parsley sprigs

With a fork, mash cream cheese until fairly smooth. Add Feta cheese and yogurt, stirring vigorously with a wooden spoon. When fairly light and fluffy, add seasonings. Cover and chill mixture for at least 2 hours.

When ready to serve, mound cheese in center of a dish. Arrange tomatoes, cucumbers, olives, and parsley around cheese. Serve with party rye or any of the thin Middle-Eastern breads. Makes 4 servings.

California Walnut Cheese Logs

1	pound soft Cheddar cheese
2	(3-ounce) packages cream cheese
¼	pound Bleu cheese
¼	pound smoked cheese
1	tablespoon prepared mustard
1	teaspoon onion, grated
3	tablespoons Port wine
	Cream
1	cup walnuts, chopped

Grate Cheddar cheese; combine with 1 package of the cream cheese, the Bleu cheese, and smoked cheese. Mix in mustard, grated onion, and port, using electric mixer or your hands. Shape into logs about an inch in diameter.

Blend remaining package of cream cheese with enough cream until spreading consistency and spread over the logs; roll in walnuts. Wrap in aluminum foil and chill in refrigerator. Slice and serve on assorted crackers. Makes 24 servings.

Potted Herb Cheese

3	cups Cheddar cheese, grated
1	tablespoon whipping cream
2	tablespoons sherry
6	tablespoons butter
1	teaspoon chives, chopped
1	teaspoon tarragon leaves
1	teaspoon sage
1	teaspoon thyme
1	teaspoon parsley flakes
	Clarified butter

Place all ingredients except clarified butter in top of a double boiler over hot water. Stir over medium heat until cheese and butter melt and mixture is thoroughly blended. Pour into pint jar; chill until cold.

Cover with a 1/4-inch deep layer of clarified butter. Cover and store in refrigerator. Let come to room temperature and serve with fingers of hot buttered toast or tiny, hot biscuits. Makes 1 pint.

Clam Savory

Cheese Rounds

1 cup biscuit mix	⅓ cup milk, approximately
½ cup sharp Cheddar cheese, grated	½ cup parsley, minced
2 tablespoons mayonnaise	1 tablespoon onion, grated

Combine first 4 ingredients, adding only enough of the milk to moisten the dough. Shape into small balls. Combine parsley and grated onion and roll balls in this mixture.

Place on a greased cookie sheet and bake in a preheated 450°F oven 8 to 10 minutes. Makes about 30 balls.

Garlic-Butter Chips

¾ cup butter or margarine   **Potato chips**
2 to 3 cloves garlic, cut into slivers

Heat butter with garlic a few minutes; remove garlic.

Brush potato chips with garlic butter; place on baking sheets lined with paper towels. Heat in a preheated 350°F oven 5 minutes; drain on clean paper towels. Yield as desired.

Plantain Chips

1 large, green plantain   **Salt (optional)**
Vegetable oil or shortening

Peel plantain and slice wafer thin (a vegetable parer works well). Heat 2 to 3 inches of vegetable oil or shortening to 375°F in heavy frying pan, or until a plantain chip dropped in will sizzle and rise to the top. Slide a few slices of plantain at a time into the hot oil for 2 to 3 minutes, or until chips turn a golden brown.

Drain on paper towels, then salt lightly. Makes about 2 cups of chips.

Tortilla Chips

1 dozen corn tortillas   **Salt**
Oil for frying

Defrost tortillas if they are frozen. Cut each tortilla into 8 wedges.

Use a small heavy skillet, electric skillet, or deep-fryer to heat at least 1 inch of cooking oil to 360°F. Fry tortilla pieces, a few at a time, until crisp and lightly browned. Remove from oil with a slotted spoon. Drain chips on paper towels and salt lightly. Serve chips with dips or refried beans. Makes 8 dozen chips.

Crumbed Mushrooms

Clam Savory

- 3 tablespoons butter
- 1 small onion, peeled and finely chopped
- ½ green pepper, finely chopped
- 1 (7½-ounce) can clams, drained and chopped
- 1 cup grated cheese
- 1 tablespoon tomato puree
- 1 tablespoon Worcestershire sauce
- 1 tablespoon sherry
- ⅛ teaspoon cayenne pepper
- Dill pickle
- 4 or 5 slices hot buttered toast

Heat butter in frying pan. Add onion and green pepper; sauté 3 minutes over low heat. Add clams, cheese, tomato puree, Worcestershire sauce, sherry, and cayenne; cook a few minutes, until cheese has melted, stirring constantly.

Put thin slice of dill pickle on each slice of toast; serve clam mixture on top. Makes 4 or 5 servings.

Favorite Egg Spread

- 12 hard-cooked eggs, riced or sieved
- 2 tablespoons butter, softened
- 4 teaspoons lemon juice
- 1½ teaspoons prepared mustard
- 2 teaspoons Worcestershire sauce
- 1 teaspoon salt
- ¼ teaspoon pepper
- About ¾ cup salad dressing
- Paprika, chives, or parsley

Combine all ingredients. Beat until smooth, adding more seasonings if desired. Refrigerate until ready to serve. Garnish with paprika, parsley, or chives. Makes 4 cups.

Hummus

- 1 or 2 cloves garlic, mashed
- ½ teaspoon salt
- ¼ teaspoon black pepper
- ¼ teaspoon paprika
- ⅛ teaspoon cayenne pepper
- 2 cups cooked garbanzo beans or chick peas (canned chick peas may be substituted, drained and rinsed and liquid reserved)
- ½ cup tahini (sesame seed paste)
- ¼ cup lemon juice
- Reserved liquid from beans as needed
- 1 tablespoon olive oil
- ½ teaspoon paprika
- Minced parsley

In a bowl, mash garlic, salt, black pepper, paprika, and cayenne pepper. Drain garbanzo beans, reserving the liquid; in a separate bowl mash thoroughly.

Gradually add garlic mixture along with tahini and lemon juice. Put in as much reserved liquid as needed to make mixture smooth, but not too runny. (Hummus should be a spreadable consistency.) Spoon into a serving bowl and pour olive oil and paprika on top. Sprinkle with parsley. Makes 2 to 2-1/2 cups.

Orange Leek Sandwich

- 6 tablespoons soft butter
- 2½ teaspoons ground coriander
- 3 slices dark rye bread
- 1 (7-ounce) can tuna, drained and flaked
- 9 pitted California ripe olives, quartered
- 1 orange, peeled and thinly sliced
- 3 teaspoons leeks, thinly sliced

Combine butter and coriander in a small bowl and blend well; spread on one side of the bread slices. Arrange tuna, olives, and orange and leek slices on bread. Cut into quarters. Makes 12 canapés.

Crumbed Mushrooms

1 pound mushrooms	3 ounces butter
1 small onion	1 egg
Salt and pepper	Packaged dry bread crumbs
2 tablespoons dry sherry	

Choose small mushrooms about the same size. Wash and trim off hard end of stems. Peel onion, chop finely, and sauté in 1/2 ounce butter until transparent. Add whole mushrooms, salt, pepper, and dry sherry; simmer gently 5 to 8 minutes. Drain and cool.

Dip in beaten egg, roll in bread crumbs, fry quickly in remaining hot butter until crisp and golden brown. Makes 4 servings.

Olive Sandwich

2 cups pitted California ripe olives, well drained	12 thin slices Monterey Jack cheese
1 large round loaf French bread, split	18 slices dry salami
Soft butter	1 large green sweet pepper, cut in rings

Slice olives. Hollow out a portion of the soft crumbs from both halves of the bread loaf and spread halves with butter. Cover bottom half with cheese, salami, green pepper, and olives and top with the remaining half of bread loaf. Wrap tightly in waxed paper and let stand in refrigerator for at least 2 hours for flavors to blend. Cut in small slices to serve. Makes 8 servings.

Party Mix

4 cups corn or rice squares	1 tablespoon Worcestershire sauce
4 cups bran or wheat squares	1 to 2 teaspoons garlic powder
4 cups unsalted small or stick pretzels	1/8 teaspoon oregano
2 cups unsalted sesame sticks	1/2 teaspoon chili powder
2 cups unsalted peanuts	1/2 teaspoon paprika
1/2 cup safflower oil	4 tablespoons Parmesan cheese

Mix all ingredients in a very large roasting pan. Bake in a 250°F oven for 1 hour. Stir and turn every 15 minutes. Makes 4 quarts.

Sweet or Salty Pretzels

Peanut Butter Ham Squares

½ cup peanut butter (smooth or crunchy)	6 thin slices boiled ham
2 teaspoons grated onion or ½ teaspoon instant minced onion	1 egg, beaten
	2 tablespoons water
	½ cup fine, dry bread crumbs
	1 cup peanut oil

Mix peanut butter and onion. Spread mixture on 1/2 the ham slices; top with remaining ham slices. Wrap in waxed paper and chill in refrigerator for about an hour. Cut into 1-inch squares.

Mix beaten egg with water. Dip squares in egg and then in bread crumbs. Fry in hot peanut oil about 2 minutes or until golden brown. Serve at once on toothpicks. Makes 5 dozen canapés.

Pistachio Puffs

1 cup water	⅓ cup Swiss cheese, shredded (medium-fine)
¼ pound (1 stick) butter	¼ cup pistachios, finely chopped
1 cup all-purpose flour	
¼ teaspoon salt	
4 large eggs	

Heat water and butter in a 2-quart saucepan over moderate heat until water boils and butter melts. Add flour and salt all at once. Remove from heat; stir vigorously until mixture leaves side of pan and begins to form a ball.

Add eggs 1 at a time, beating well after each addition; continue to beat until mixture is smooth and glossy. Stir in cheese and pistachios.

Drop by rounded tablespoonfuls, about 1-inch apart, onto a large, greased cookie sheet. Bake in preheated 400°F oven until golden brown, 40 to 45 minutes. Serve at once. Makes 15 puffs.

Note: You can bake the pistachio puffs ahead and, appropriately wrapped, store them in the freezer. At serving time, unwrap and place the frozen puffs on a cookie sheet; heat in a fairly hot oven just until thawed and surface is crisp; serve at once.

Quark Snacks

Herbed Pistachios

1 cup shelled pistachios	⅛ teaspoon each thyme and oregano, crushed
2 tablespoons butter	1 tablespoon parsley, minced

Melt butter in skillet. Add herbs and pistachios; toss to coat.
Sauté about 5 minutes, or until pistachios are coated and crisp. Cool on paper towels. Makes 1 cup.

Cajun Popcorn

- 1 teaspoon paprika
- ½ teaspoon onion powder
- ½ teaspoon garlic powder
- ¼ teaspoon cayenne pepper
- 1 teaspoon lemon pepper
- 2½ quarts popped popcorn
- ¼ to ½ cup butter, melted

Combine all spices in a cup; mix well. Pour melted butter over warm popcorn, mixing through carefully. Sprinkle spices over popcorn and quickly toss.

Spread popcorn on a nonstick cookie sheet. Bake at 300°F for 10 minutes. Cool and store in airtight container. Makes 2-1/2 quarts.

Sweet or Salty Pretzels

- 1 package dry yeast
- ½ cup lukewarm milk
- 4 or more cups of flour
- 1 teaspoon sugar
- ½ teaspoon salt
- 2 egg yolks
- ½ pound butter
- 2 tablespoons kosher salt or 4 tablespoons fine sugar

Dissolve yeast in lukewarm milk. Put flour in a large bowl, making a depression in the center. Add dissolved yeast and milk, sugar, and salt. Add 1 egg yolk and mix well.

Liberally dot the mixture with 1/4 pound of butter; knead it quickly and lightly. Roll out dough on a floured board to a large square. Dot this with the other 1/4 pound of butter. Cover dough and set it in the refrigerator for 15 minutes.

Put dough on flour-covered work surface and roll it out again to a square. The butter should now be worked into the batter. Knead dough 4 times and let it rest in refrigerator. Repeat this process again. Then let dough rest for 30 minutes at room temperature. Roll out dough for the final time to about 1 inch thick and 10 inches long, so that you can cut sticks about 1 inch wide. Cut and form these sticks into pretzel shapes. Put them onto a greased cookie sheet.

Brush pretzels with egg yolk. Then sprinkle them with coarse salt or sugar, according to your taste. Bake pretzels at 425°F for 20 minutes. Allow them to cool before serving. Makes 18 or 19 pretzels.

Sausage and Apple Snack

Party Snacks/21

Quark Snacks

2 cups all-purpose white flour	**Cottage-Cheese Filling**
3 teaspoons baking powder	1 cup dry-curd cottage cheese
1 teaspoon salt	2 tablespoons dried parsley flakes
¼ cup all-vegetable shortening	1 teaspoon salt
¾ cup milk (about)	2 tablespoons pimiento, chopped
2 egg yolks, beaten	
3 tablespoons caraway seeds	

Combine dry ingredients; cut in shortening to resemble coarse meal. Add milk to form soft dough. Knead dough 6 times. Roll on floured surface to 1/4 inch thick. Brush half the biscuits with egg yolks; sprinkle with caraway seeds. Bake biscuits at 450°F 10 minutes or until golden brown.

Make cottage-cheese filling by combining cottage cheese, parsley flakes, salt, and pimiento. To serve, spread filling on plain biscuits; top with caraway-seed biscuits. Makes 20 snacks.

Sausage and Apple Snacks

1 pound sausage meat	2 tablespoons flour
2 tablespoons parsley, chopped	Butter
½ teaspoon curry powder	2 dessert apples
½ teaspoon mixed herbs	6 thin slices bacon
Salt and pepper	Few sprigs parsley
	Toast

Combine sausage, parsley, curry powder, herbs, and seasoning; shape into 6 patties. Coat lightly with flour; fry each side in butter about 5 minutes. Remove from pan; keep hot.

Core but do not peel apples; cut each into 3 slices. Fry each side about 2 minutes.

Roll up bacon; put onto skewer. Fry or broil.

Put patties on serving dish with apple ring on top. Arrange bacon rolls in center; garnish with parsley. Serve with hot toast. Makes 6 servings.

Polish Sausage Links

Berry-Filled Melon

Polish Sausage Links

1½ cups all-purpose white flour	½ cup butter
1 (3-ounce) package cream cheese, softened	6 Polish sausage links
	1 egg yolk, beaten

Combine flour, cream cheese, and butter; mix until a soft dough forms. Divide dough into 7 equal parts. Wrap each link in dough.

Cut remaining dough into crescent shapes. Place crescents on top of wrapped Polish links; press to secure. Brush each wrapped link with beaten egg yolk. Bake in 425°F oven 10 to 12 minutes or until golden brown. Slice to serve. Makes 6 servings.

Sweet Snacks

Yogurt Cocktails

1 medium can sliced peaches	1 small can pineapple chunks
1 cup quartered seedless grapes	½ cup cream, whipped (optional)
2 (8-ounce) cartons yogurt	4 maraschino cherries
2 pears, peeled and sliced	

Reserve 8 peach slices for decoration. Place a layer of grapes in 4 parfait glasses. Cover with a layer of yogurt, then add layers of pears, peaches, and pineapple alternately with yogurt until the last layer of yogurt comes within 3/4 inch of the top of each glass.

Pipe a spiral of whipped cream over the yogurt in each glass, then top with a cherry. Push 2 reserved peach slices onto each glass. Makes 4 servings.

Chocolate Covered Anything

6 ounces semisweet chocolate	Pretzels
3 tablespoons shortening	Dried fruits

Melt chocolate with shortening in top of double boiler, stirring until just melted. Keep over hot water and remove from heat. Using a fork, dip pretzel or fruit 1 at a time in sauce. Lightly tap excess sauce off on the side of the pot.

Spray a wire rack with no-stick or lightly grease it. Dry on the rack with a piece of waxed paper under it. You can dip 1/2 the pretzel or fruit if you wish or the whole thing. Makes enough to coat 2 pounds of fruit or about 60 pretzels.

Blind Dates

1 package dried dates   Sugar
Salted cashews or peanuts, or a
 mixture

Cut a slit in each date and remove the stone. Fill each date with 1 or more nuts and roll in granulated sugar. Pack in tins using waxed paper between layers.

Quick Energy Pickups

3 or 4 graham crackers	½ cup instant nonfat dry milk
1 cup powdered sugar	3 teaspoons water
1 cup crunchy peanut butter	
1 cup semisweet chocolate chips	

With your fingers, crush graham crackers onto a sheet of waxed paper.

Mix remaining ingredients thoroughly in bowl. Shape mixture into 1-inch balls. Roll balls in graham cracker crumbs until coated.

Arrange coated balls on ungreased cookie sheet and refrigerate for about 20 minutes. Makes 30 snacks.

Melon à la Mode

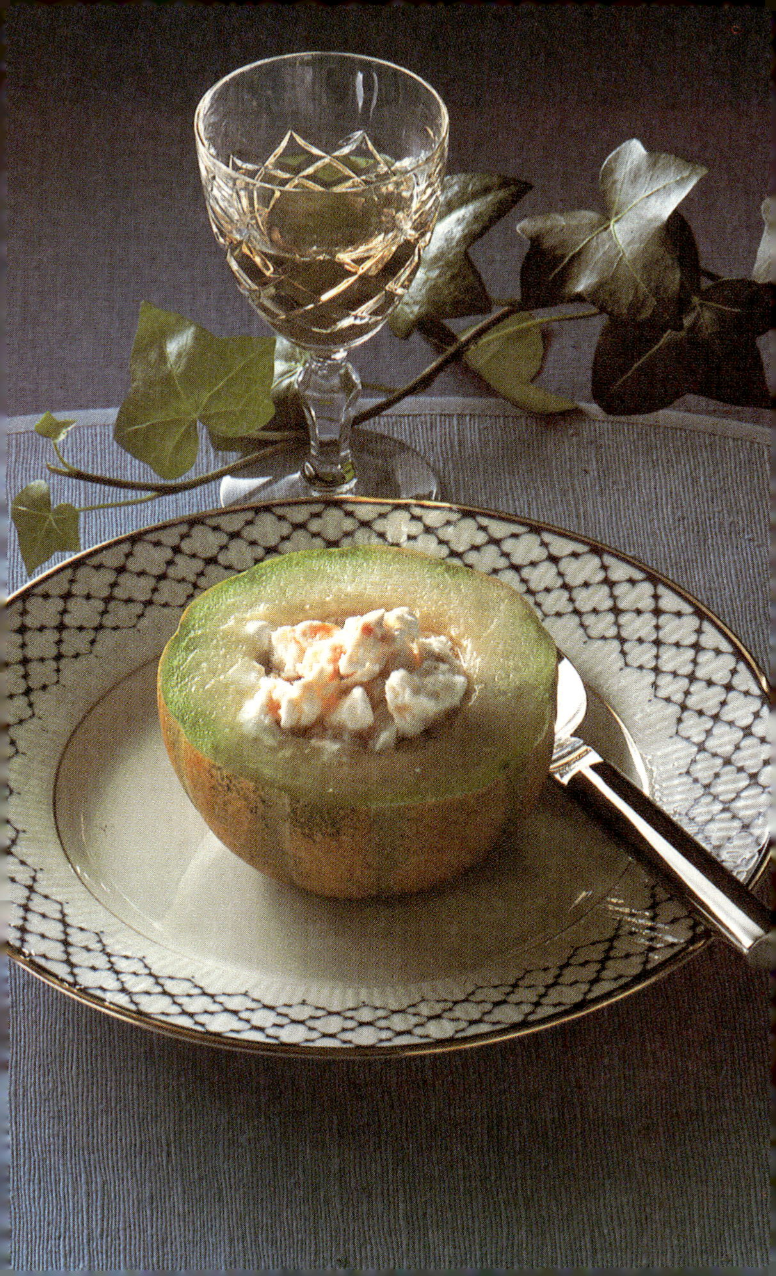

Berry-Filled Melon

½ small honeydew melon	1 teaspoon sugar
3 to 4 tablespoons red berries, for example wild strawberries and currants (preferably 2 kinds)	Several drops calvados

Cut melon in half and fill with berries. Sprinkle sugar on top. Moisten with a few drops of calvados. Makes 1 serving.

Melon à la Mode

2 cantaloupes	4 tablespoons good brandy
8 tablespoons nougat ice-cream	

Wash melons, cut them in half, and remove seeds. Put melon halves on serving plates.

Just before serving, place 2 spoonfuls of the ice cream in each melon half and pour a tablespoon of brandy on top. Makes 4 servings.

Pears in Chocolate Sauce

1 (29-ounce) can pear halves	1 tablespoon butter
8 ounces semisweet chocolate	1 egg yolk
2 tablespoons hot water	½ cup heavy cream
	1 egg white

Drain pear halves; arrange in 6 individual serving dishes.

Place chocolate in top of double boiler. Stir in hot water; melt chocolate over boiling water. Remove from heat. Stir in butter until melted. Add egg yolk and heavy cream. Beat egg white until stiff peaks form; fold into chocolate sauce. Spoon chocolate sauce over pears. Serve immediately. Makes 6 servings.

Pears in Chocolate Sauce

Butterscotch Brownies

¼	cup butter	1	teaspoon baking powder
1	cup light brown sugar	½	teaspoon salt
1	egg	½	teaspoon vanilla
¾	cup flour, sifted	½	cup walnuts, chopped

Melt butter. Combine with brown sugar. Cool.

Stir in egg and sifted dry ingredients. Add vanilla and nuts. Spread in well-greased, 8-inch square pan. Bake in 350°F oven 20 to 25 minutes. Cut into bars while still warm. Makes 1-1/2 dozen.

Chocolate Balls

3	squares unsweetened baking chocolate	¼	cup sugar
1	tablespoon strong black coffee	1	egg yolk
1	cup (2 sticks) butter or margarine	1	cup walnuts or pecans, chopped
		1	tablespoon rum
		2½	cups flour

Break chocolate into small pieces. Put with coffee into double boiler; stir until melted. Let cool.

Cream butter and sugar until light and fluffy. Beat in egg yolk. Add nuts and rum. Stir in cooled chocolate. Add sifted flour; blend to smooth dough. Wrap in foil. Chill 1 hour.

Form teaspoons of dough into balls. Roll well in sugar. Arrange on well-greased baking sheets, leaving space between for them to spread. Press half a nut into each ball. In a preheated 350°F oven, bake about 15 minutes. Makes about 40 small cookies.

Peanut-Butter Nuggets

1	cup peanut butter	1½	cups (1 can) condensed milk
1	teaspoon lemon juice	1	cup seedless raisins, chopped
¼	teaspoon salt		

Mix peanut butter, lemon juice, and salt together. Gradually stir in milk. Add raisins. Drop by teaspoon onto greased baking sheets. Bake in a preheated 375°F oven 10 minutes. Makes about 36.

Sweet Snacks/31

Hussar's Kisses

Chocolate-Delight Bars

- ½ cup butter
- 1 egg yolk
- 2 tablespoons water
- 1¼ cups flour
- 1 teaspoon sugar
- 1 teaspoon baking powder
- 1 (12-ounce) package chocolate morsels
- 2 eggs
- ¾ cup sugar
- 6 tablespoons butter
- 2 teaspoons vanilla
- 2 cups nuts, finely chopped

Beat 1/2 cup butter, egg yolk, and water together. Sift and stir in flour, sugar, and baking powder. Press into 13 × 9 × 2-inch greased pan. Bake in a preheated 350°F oven 10 minutes. Remove from oven.

Sprinkle with morsels. Return to oven 1 minute; remove. Spread chocolate over top.

Beat 2 eggs until thick. Beat in 3/4 cup sugar. Stir in 6 tablespoons melted butter and vanilla. Spread on top of chocolate layer. Sprinkle chopped nuts on top. Bake at 350°F 30 to 35 minutes. Cut into 1-1/2 inch squares. Makes 2 dozen.

Chocolate-Wine Cookies

- 1½ cups all-purpose flour
- 1 teaspoon baking powder
- ½ teaspoon cinnamon
- 1 egg, beaten
- 1 cup pecans, ground
- ½ cup butter, softened
- ½ cup sugar
- 1 teaspoon sherry
- 1 (6-ounce) package chocolate chips, melted
- Almond slivers

Sift flour, baking powder, and cinnamon together onto a clean working surface, then shape into a ring. Place egg, pecans, butter, sugar, sherry, and 1/2 cup of melted chocolate in the center. Blend mixture with pastry scrapers until a smooth dough is formed.

Roll dough out on a floured surface to 1/8-inch thickness. Cut into circles with a 1-1/2-inch cookie cutter. Press circles into miniature cupcake pans, forming a very shallow shell. Bake in a preheated 350°F oven for about 20 to 22 minutes. Cool on a wire rack.

Fill centers with remaining melted chocolate. Insert an almond sliver in each dab of chocolate. Chill for 5 minutes to set chocolate. Makes about 3-1/2 dozen cookies.

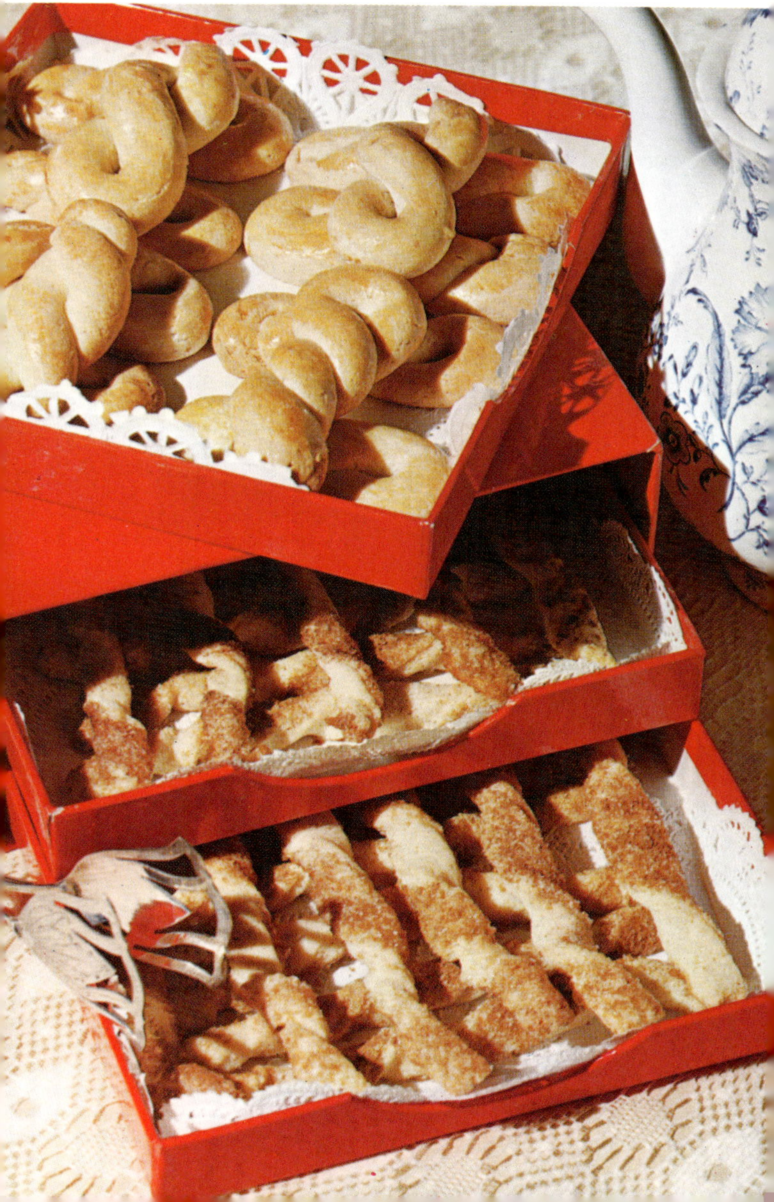

Hartshorns

¼ pound butter or margarine	2 teaspoons baking soda
4 eggs	4½ cups flour
1 cup sugar	Fat for deep frying
½ lemon rind, grated	
½ teaspoon ground cardamom	

Melt butter. Let cool. Beat eggs and sugar together. Add butter, lemon rind, cardamom, baking soda, and flour; mix well. Place in refrigerator to chill overnight.

Roll small lumps of dough into strips 6 inches long and as thick as your little finger. Form each strip into a ring. Cook rings in deep fat until golden brown. Drain well on paper towels. Store in sealed tin. Makes 36 hartshorns.

Hussar's Kisses

½ cup butter or margarine	2 egg whites, lightly beaten
¼ cup sugar	1¼ cups ground or grated blanched almonds (walnuts or other nuts may be substituted)
2 egg yolks	
2 teaspoons lemon juice	
½ teaspoon lemon rind, grated	
1½ cups all-purpose flour (do not sift)	Apricot or plum jam or canned leckvar (poppy-seed) filling

Cream butter and sugar until light. Add egg yolks, lemon juice, and lemon rind; mix well. Thoroughly blend in flour. Refrigerate dough 2 hours.

Using teaspoon of dough for each cookie, form into 1-inch balls. Dip in egg white; roll in nuts. Place 1 inch apart on ungreased cookie sheets. Indent top of each cookie with your thumb to form small hollow. If using leckvar, fill hollows with 1/2 teaspoon filling before baking. Bake in preheated 375°F oven 10 minutes or until lightly browned. Remove from cookie sheet; if using jam, fill hollows now. Allow to cool on rack. Makes 2-1/2 to 3 dozen cookies.

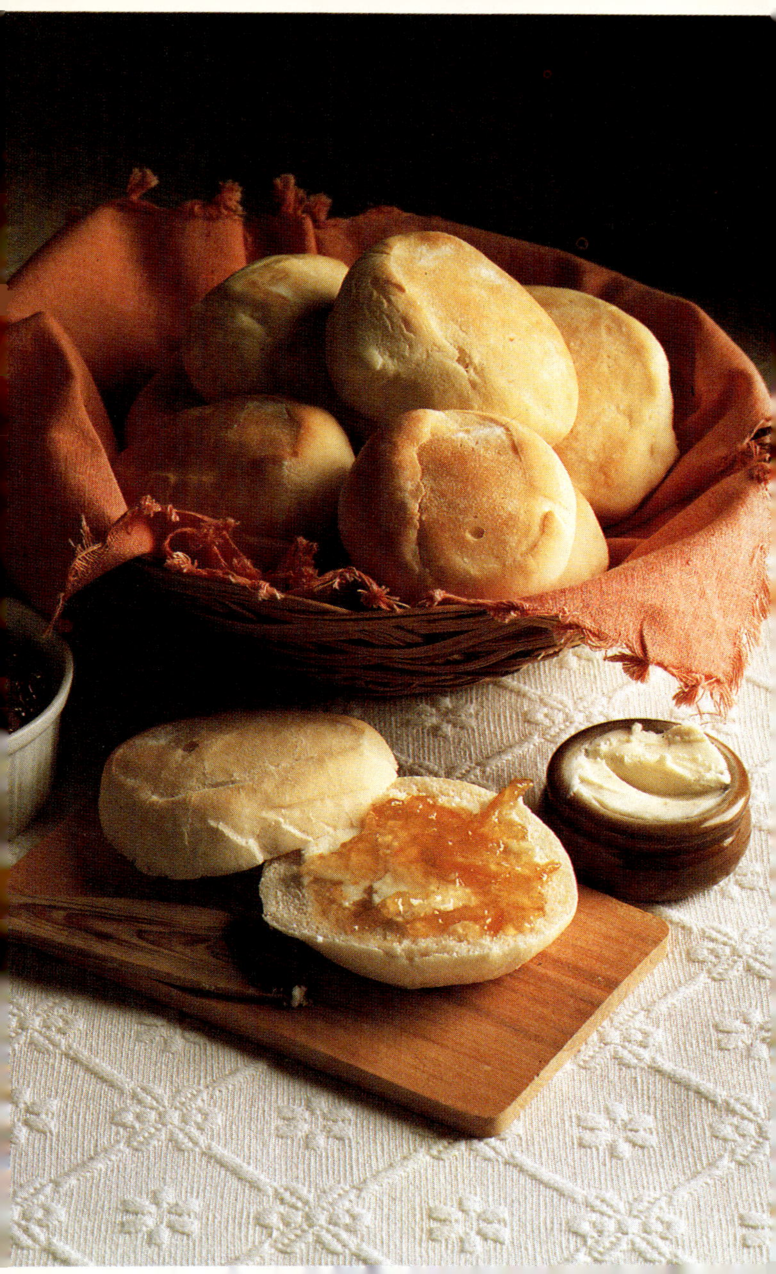

Pretzel Cookies

- ½ cup (1 stick) butter or margarine
- ¾ cup granulated sugar
- 2 eggs, beaten
- 2 tablespoons milk
- 1 cup flour
- ¼ teaspoon salt
- ½ cup brown sugar
- 2 tablespoons ground cinnamon

Cream butter with 1/4 cup granulated sugar. Add eggs and milk; beat until smooth. Add flour and salt sifted together; mix to smooth dough. Wrap in foil. Chill 2 to 3 hours.

Mix brown sugar, cinnamon, and remaining granulated sugar together. Sprinkle mixture onto pastry board. Put dough on board. Roll out to about 1/4 inch thick. Cut dough into strips about 1/2 inch wide. Form into twists. Sprinkle well with sugar mixture.

Arrange on greased and floured baking sheets. In a preheated 375°F oven, bake 12 minutes or until just delicately browned. Makes about 36 cookies.

Walnut Rum Cookies

- 1 cup walnuts, chopped
- 2 tablespoons cocoa
- ¼ cup rum or bourbon
- 2 cups vanilla wafers, finely crushed
- 3 tablespoons white corn syrup
- 2 cups confectioners' sugar

Mix all ingredients except sugar. Form into balls. Roll in sugar. Makes 30 to 35 cookies.

Jam Slices

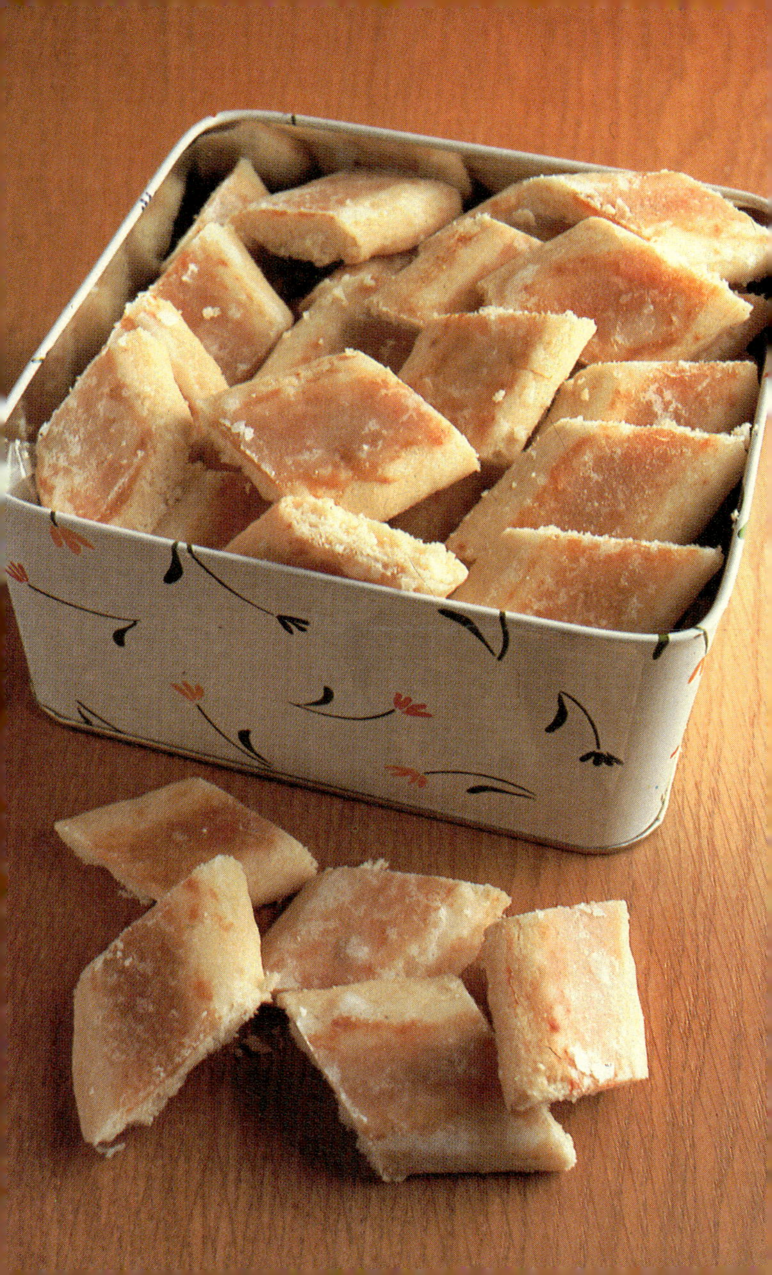

Breads

Apple Bread

2 tablespoons butter	1 package active dry yeast
¾ cup sugar	¾ cup warm water
1 teaspoon cinnamon	1 teaspoon salt
1 apple, peeled and thinly sliced	2¼ cups flour, sifted
A few raisins	1 egg
	¼ cup shortening

Melt butter in a 9×9-inch baking pan. Mix 1/2 cup of sugar and cinnamon in a small bowl. Sprinkle sugar mixture on melted butter. Arrange apple slices in rows on sugar mixture in pan. Sprinkle with a few raisins.

Stir yeast and water together in a large bowl. Add remaining 1/4 cup of sugar, salt, and 1 cup of flour. Beat 2 minutes or until batter drops in sheets from beater or spoon. Add egg, shortening, and remaining 1-1/4 cups of flour; beat until smooth.

Drop batter by small spoonfuls over apples and raisins in pan. Cover pan and let rise 50 to 60 minutes, or until double in size. Bake at 375°F for 30 to 35 minutes, or until brown. Immediately remove bread from pan by inverting it onto a serving plate. Makes 1 loaf.

Banana Bread

1¾ cups unsifted flour	2 eggs
1 tablespoon baking powder	1 cup bananas, mashed
½ teaspoon salt	½ cup walnuts, chopped
¾ cup sugar	(optional)
½ cup shortening	

Grease a 9 × 5-inch pan.

Mix flour, baking powder, and salt thoroughly. Beat sugar, shortening, and eggs together until light and fluffy. Mix in bananas. Add the dry ingredients; stir just until smooth. Pour into prepared pan.

Bake in a preheated 350°F oven until firmly set when lightly touched in the center, 50 to 60 minutes. (Bread may crack across the top.) Cool on a rack. Remove from pan after 10 minutes. Makes 1 loaf.

Hard Rye Bread Wafers

Walnut Brown Bread

Apricot Nut Bread

- 1 cup boiling water
- 1 cup dried apricots, chopped
- 3 cups unsifted flour
- 1 tablespoon baking powder
- ½ teaspoon salt
- ⅓ cup butter or margarine
- 1 cup sugar
- 2 eggs
- ½ cup light corn syrup
- 1 cup nuts, chopped

Grease and lightly flour a 9×5×3-inch loaf pan. Pour water over apricots and let stand 15 minutes. Stir flour, baking powder, and salt together.

In a large bowl, mix butter, sugar, eggs, and corn syrup until smooth and well blended. Mix in apricot mixture and nuts. Gradually mix in dry ingredients.

Pour mixture into pan. Bake in a 350°F oven about 1-1/4 hours or until a cake tester inserted in center of loaf comes out clean. Cool in pan 10 minutes. Remove from pan and cool on a rack. Serve with jam or jelly, if desired. Makes 1 loaf.

Cheddar Cheese Bread

- ½ cup warm water
- 2 (¼-ounce) packages dry yeast, or 2 (0.6-ounce) cakes compressed yeast
- 2 tablespoons sugar
- 1 cup milk, scalded, or ½ cup evaporated milk and ½ cup hot water
- 2 tablespoons shortening
- 2 teaspoons salt
- 5 cups unbleached flour, divided
- 2 cups natural sharp Cheddar cheese spread
- Melted butter

Dissolve yeast and 1 teaspoon of sugar in water in a small bowl. Let stand for 5 to 10 minutes, or until mixture expands and becomes bubbly. Set it aside.

Combine shortening, remaining sugar, and salt with milk in a large bowl. Stir until shortening melts. Stir in 1 cup of flour; add cheese. Add reserved yeast mixture. Gradually stir in enough of the remaining flour to make a stiff dough.

Turn out onto a lightly floured board. Knead 8 to 10 minutes, or until the dough is smooth and elastic. Dust board and dough with more flour if necessary to prevent sticking.

Shape into a ball. Place in a large greased bowl. Turn to grease the ball on all sides. Cover and let it rise in a warm draft-free place for 1 hour, or until doubled in bulk.

Punch down the dough. Turn out on a lightly floured board. Cover and let it rise for 10 minutes. Cut dough in half and shape into 2 loaves. Grease 2 (8-1/2 × 4-1/2 × 2-5/8-inch) loaf pans.

Place dough in pans. Cover and let rise in a warm, draft-free place for 30 minutes, or until dough has risen to rim of pans.

Bake at 375°F for 35 minutes, or until crust is brown and top sounds hollow when tapped. Remove from pans. Cool on racks. Brush tops lightly with melted butter. Makes 2 loaves.

Date-Nut Loaf

- 3 cups flour
- 4 tablespoons baking powder
- ½ cup sugar
- 1 teaspoon salt
- 1 cup dates, chopped
- ¼ cup pecans, chopped
- 1 beaten egg
- 1½ cups milk
- 2 tablespoons butter, melted
- Slivered nuts (optional)

Place dry ingredients in a large bowl and add dates and nuts. Beat egg, milk, and butter together and gradually add to flour mixture. When all is mixed, turn into a buttered loaf pan and allow to stand for 30 minutes. Bake at 350°F for about 1-1/2 hours. Cool loaf on a rack. Decorate with slivered nuts. Slice to serve—the thinner the better. Makes about 10 slices.

Drop Doughnuts

- ¼ cup soft butter
- 1 cup sugar
- 2 egg yolks, beaten
- 1 whole egg, beaten
- 4 cups flour
- 2 teaspoons baking powder
- ¼ teaspoon nutmeg
- ½ teaspoon soda
- ¾ cup buttermilk
- Powdered sugar

Cream butter and sugar. Stir in egg yolks and whole egg; blend. In a separate bowl, sift all dry ingredients together except powdered sugar; add to creamed mixture, alternating with buttermilk. Stir to mix all ingredients.

Cook by dropping spoonfuls of dough into 375°F deep fat. Fry a few at a time, to keep fat temperature constant. Turn to brown on all sides. Drain on paper towels; sprinkle with powdered sugar. Makes 36 doughnuts.

French Buns

5¼ tablespoons margarine or butter	2 cakes compressed yeast
2 cups milk	2 teaspoons salt
	5⅔ to 6 cups flour

Melt butter in a pot. Add milk and allow mixture to become finger temperature (98.6F). Mix yeast in a small amount of milk mixture, and then pour over rest of milk. Add most of flour and salt. Work into a smooth dough and let rise in a draft-free place for about 40 minutes.

Knead dough on a baking table. Divide dough into 4 parts. Roll each dough piece out into a long roll and cut each roll into 8 pieces. Dip pieces in rest of flour. Place them on a greased baking sheet. Let rise for about 30 minutes.

Bake in a hot oven, 425° to 450°F, for about 8 to 10 minutes. Serve with marmalade. Makes 32 buns.

Fruit Loaf

2 cups mixed dried fruits, finely chopped	¾ cup sugar
1½ cups all-purpose flour, sifted	¾ cup butter
3 teaspoons baking powder	2 eggs, beaten
½ teaspoon salt	1 tablespoon milk
	¼ teaspoon almond extract

Soak dried fruits in enough boiling water to cover for 10 minutes, then drain well. Sift flour, baking powder, salt, and sugar together into a mixing bowl. Cut in butter with a pastry blender until mixture is the consistency of fine bread crumbs. Stir in dried fruits until evenly distributed. Add eggs, milk, and almond extract and beat thoroughly. The batter will be very stiff.

Spread batter in a well-greased loaf pan. Bake in a preheated 350°F oven for 1 hour, or until bread tests done. Cool slightly, then remove from pan. Serve warm with butter, if desired. Makes 10 to 12 servings.

Jam Slices

- 1⅔ cups flour
- ¼ cup sugar
- 14 tablespoons margarine or butter, at room temperature
- ⅓ cup jam or applesauce
- ⅔ cup confectioners' sugar
- ½ tablespoon water

Place flour and sugar in a food processor. Divide margarine or butter into 6 to 8 pieces and add to flour and sugar. Using plastic mixer attachment, start the machine; let mixture blend for 20 to 30 seconds. Let dough stand in a cold place for about an hour.

Roll dough out into 4, flat, long-shaped buns and place them on a baking sheet lined with baking paper. Make a depression down middle of buns; fill with jam or applesauce. Bake in the middle of a preheated 400°F oven for about 10 minutes. Let buns cool on baking sheet.

Mix confectioners' sugar and water together. Brush it over buns and cut them into slanted slices. Makes about 60 slices.

Hard Rye Bread Wafers

- 1½ cakes compressed yeast
- 2 cups water, at 98.6°F
- 3 cups coarse rye flour
- 2 cups flour
- 2½ teaspoons salt
- 1 teaspoon sugar for the rising process
- 2 teaspoons caraway

Crumble yeast into a large bowl and dissolve it in 98.6°F water. Add remaining ingredients and work together into a smooth dough. Sprinkle with a little flour, cover with a baking cloth, and let rise for about 30 minutes.

Knead dough and roll it out so that it is very, very thin (less than 1/16 inch thick). Cut out large, round "cookies" with the help of a plate that is about 7 inches in diameter. Prick dough with a fork, place rounds on a baking sheet, spread a baking cloth over them, and let rise for about 20 minutes.

Preheat oven to 400°F while dough is rising. Bake for 5 minutes. Turn slices over and bake for another 5 minutes. Makes about 25 slices.

Cheese-Croissant Bake

Walnut Brown Bread

1 cup all-purpose flour, sifted	1 (6-ounce) can evaporated milk
½ cup sugar	½ cup water
2 teaspoons soda	1 tablespoon vinegar
½ teaspoon salt	1 egg, well beaten
1½ cups graham flour	1 cup dark molasses
1½ cups walnuts, coarsely chopped	Maple syrup

Sift flour, sugar, soda, and salt together in a large mixing bowl, then stir in graham flour and 1 cup walnuts. Mix milk and water, then stir in vinegar; add to flour mixture. Add egg and molasses and beat until well mixed.

Place in a greased loaf pan. Bake in a preheated 325°F oven for 1 hour and 15 minutes, or until bread tests done. Cool for 10 minutes, then remove from pan. Place on wire rack and cool completely. Brush top lightly with maple syrup, then sprinkle remaining walnuts over the syrup. Wrap in aluminum foil and store for at least 24 hours before serving. Makes about 9 servings.

Light Meals

Cheese-Croissant Bake

3 eggs	¼ cup fine soft bread crumbs
1 egg yolk	½ teaspoon onion salt
3 cups milk	⅛ teaspoon white pepper
¾ cup Parmesan cheese, freshly grated	6 stale croissants

Place eggs and egg yolk in large bowl and beat until well blended. Pour milk into a saucepan and bring just to boiling point. Stir a small amount of milk into eggs, then add remaining milk gradually, stirring constantly. Stir in cheese, bread crumbs, and seasonings.

Place the croissants in a deep, 6-cup soufflé dish and pour egg mixture over croissants. Let stand at room temperature for 1 hour or until the croissants are soaked. Bake in a preheated 375°F oven for 7 minutes. Reduce oven temperature to 325°F and bake for about 1 hour longer or until the egg mixture is set. Makes 6 servings.

Curry Spiced Egg

- 8 eggs
- 1 large onion
- 1 tablespoon margarine
- 1 tablespoon curry
- 1¼ cups chicken broth
- ½ teaspoon salt
- ¼ teaspoon black pepper
- 2½ teaspoons arrowroot flour
- ⅓ cup crème fraîche
- Juice from ½ lemon

Hard-boil eggs for 10 minutes. Meanwhile, peel onion and finely chop it. Melt margarine in a saucepan; add curry and onion. Cook onion so that it slowly softens over low heat for several minutes. Add chicken broth, salt, and pepper and simmer for about 10 minutes.

Mix crème fraîche with arrowroot and lemon juice and fold into sauce. Bring to a boil quickly, then pour sauce over eggs, which have been shelled and cut in half. Sprinkle a little parsley on top, if desired. Makes 4 servings.

Caraway Biscuits with Ham Filling

- 1 (10-ounce) package pie-crust mix or enough homemade pie pastry for 2 crusts
- ½ cup Swiss cheese, shredded
- 4 tablespoons cold water (approximately)
- 1 egg, well beaten
- 1 tablespoon caraway seeds

Ham Filling
- 1¼ cups cooked ham, ground or finely minced
- ¼ cup mayonnaise
- ¼ cup celery, finely minced
- 1½ teaspoons freeze-dried chives
- ½ teaspoon prepared mustard

Combine pie-crust mix (or homemade pastry) and Swiss cheese in mixing bowl; mix well. Sprinkle cold water over mix; stir with fork until mixture is just dampened. Form into ball. If mixture will not hold together, add small amount cold water.

Divide dough into 2 parts; roll 1 part at a time on pastry cloth or lightly floured surface to 1/4 inch thick. Cut into 1-1/2-inch rounds (approximately 40). Place on ungreased cookie sheets. Brush half of rounds with egg; sprinkle lightly with caraway seeds. Bake in preheated 375°F oven 10 to 12 minutes or until lightly browned. Place on rack to cool.

Combine all filling ingredients; mix well. Place heaping teaspoons of mixture on plain pie-crust rounds; top each with caraway-seed-topped round. Arrange biscuits on platter; garnish with parsley and cherry tomatoes. Makes approximately 20.

Note: Pie-crust rounds can be made in advance and stored in air-tight container until ready for use.

Light Meals/49

Curry Spiced Egg

Cheese Pie

Pastry
- 14 tablespoons butter
- 1⅔ cups flour
- 3 tablespoons water

Filling
- ⅔ cup light cream
- ⅔ cup sour cream
- 4 eggs
- ⅓ cup Parmesan cheese, grated
- ¼ teaspoon black pepper
- 1 teaspoon salt
- ½ teaspoon paprika
- 1 cup aged Cheddar cheese, cubed
- 1 cup Swiss cheese, cubed
- ⅓ cup onion, minced

Combine all pastry ingredients in a bowl. Mix dough together using your fingertips until it is well blended. Let stand in a cool place for about 1/2 hour.

Preheat oven to 425°F. Flatten dough with palm of your hand into a thin baking dish with a detachable bottom (with a diameter of 11 inches) so that the bottom and sides of the dish are evenly covered. Make sure that the dough goes all the way up to the edge of the baking dish and that there are no holes in the dough. Place dish in oven and bake pie shell for about 10 minutes.

Meanwhile, mix cream, sour cream, and eggs together and beat well. Season with grated Parmesan cheese, salt, pepper, and paprika. Combine and lay out the 2 kinds of cheese in the pie shell. Sprinkle minced onion on top. Finally, pour egg mixture over cheese cubes and place pie on a rack in the middle of the oven. Bake for 35 minutes. If pie gets too dark, cover top with a piece of aluminum foil. Makes 6 servings.

Herb and Cottage Cheese Pie

Pie Crust
- 5¼ tablespoons butter
- Salt
- 1½ cups all-purpose flour, sifted
- 1 egg yolk
- 1 tablespoon cold water

Filling
- 2 leeks
- 2 tablespoons butter
- 1 package frozen or 1½ pounds fresh spinach
- 2 tablespoons parsley, chopped
- 2 tablespoons chives, chopped
- Salt
- Pepper
- 3 eggs, separated
- ⅓ pound cottage cheese

First make pie crust. Place butter in a warm bowl, and soften butter with a wooden spoon. Add salt to the flour and shape it into a pyramid in the bowl. Make a hole in the middle and fill it with butter, egg yolk, another dash of salt, and water; stir with a spoon. Dip your fingers in a small amount

Cheese Pie

of flour and knead the dough. Add more water, if needed. Place dough in a piece of waxed paper so that it is totally covered; refrigerate. Remove dough from refrigerator 15 minutes before it is to be rolled out.

Cut white part of leeks into thin rings. Melt butter in a frying pan, and place leek rings in the butter. Stir until they have become soft. Add spinach and the herbs. Season well and mix. Add more melted butter if mixture seems too dry. Let cool.

Roll out dough and line a pie tin with detachable sides or 4 individual tart pans with it. Cut away any extras around the edge with a sharp knife.

Preheat oven to 375°F. Cover a baking sheet with foil and place it in the oven. Place herb mixture in the bottom of the forms. Separate egg yolks and whites. Strain cottage cheese through a sieve; beat egg yolks and cottage cheese together and season well. Beat whites into stiff peaks and fold them carefully into cheese mixture. Pour into pie forms.

Bake for about 30 minutes until pie has risen and becomes golden brown. Serve warm or cold. Makes 6 servings.

Herb and Cottage Cheese Pie

Basque Omelette

- 6 eggs
- ¼ cup light cream
- 1 red pepper
- 1 green pepper
- 1 onion
- 1 clove garlic
- ½ cup ham, cut into julienne-strips
- 3 sprigs fresh parsley, chopped
- ⅛ pound butter
- Salt to taste

In a large bowl, stir eggs with a fork; add cream and salt. In a large frying pan, melt butter over medium heat. Add egg mixture, stirring often with a wooden spoon. Immediately add chopped vegetables and ham. Continue stirring until eggs are cooked; remove from heat. Add chopped parsley, and serve. Makes 4 servings.

Eggs on Potato Cakes

1 pound potatoes	5 eggs
Salt and pepper	Pinch of nutmeg
2 tablespoons butter or margarine	Oil or lard for frying

Peel potatoes and cook in boiling salted water. When tender drain them thoroughly. Beat 1 egg with nutmeg. Mash potatoes (leftover mashed potatoes will do well) and beat in butter, seasoning, beaten egg, and nutmeg. Shape dough into 4 potato cakes.

Heat a little oil or fat in a frying pan and fry potato cakes until golden. Fry the 4 remaining eggs and serve them on top of potato cakes. Makes 4 servings.

Gem Beef Tidbits

¼ pound ground beef	¼ teaspoon chili powder
½ teaspoon salad oil	¼ teaspoon Tabasco sauce
2 tablespoons onion, finely chopped	1 (8-ounce) can gem flake rolls
2 tablespoons chili sauce	Grated American cheese
½ teaspoon salt	

In a small skillet, brown meat in oil. Stir in onion, chili sauce, salt, chili powder, and Tabasco sauce. Cook until onion is tender but not browned; remove from heat. With fingers, separate each roll in half. Use the palm of the hand or the bottom of a glass to flatten each half-roll into a round or clam shape until it is twice its original size. Place 2 rounded teaspoonfuls meat mixture in center of half of the flattened roll halves.

With a sharp knife, cut a cross in center of remaining roll halves. Pull back cut corners to open center of each. Place 1 cut half atop each meat-filled half. Seal edges by pressing together with tines of a fork. Sprinkle tops with cheese.

Place each on ungreased cookie sheet. Bake in 375°F oven for 12 to 14 minutes, or until lightly browned. Serve piping hot. Makes 12 servings.

Filled Pancakes

2 eggs	⅓ cup parsley, finely chopped
1 cup flour	
2 cups milk	1¼ cups sour cream
¼ teaspoon salt	½ teaspoon salt
1 tablespoon margarine	¼ teaspoon lemon pepper
	¼ teaspoon Italian salad spice
Filling	1 teaspoon French mustard
½ pound fresh mushrooms	¼ pound cheese, freshly grated
¾ pound smoked ham	
1 leek	

Make a smooth pancake batter by beating together eggs, flour, and 2/3 cup of milk. Then add rest of milk and salt.

Make pancakes, allowing 3 pancakes per person. As pancakes are done, place one on top of the other. Preheat oven to 475°F.

Rinse and slice mushrooms. Cut ham into small, fine cubes and the leek into thin slices; chop parsley. Mix sour cream and spices together. Blend carefully, as sour cream will become thin if it is stirred too vigorously. Fill pancakes with chopped ingredients and sour cream, roll them up, and place them on an ovenproof plate.

Cover with grated cheese and bake on the top rack of a 475°F oven for 10 to 12 minutes. The pancakes can be made several hours before dinner if you wish to prepare the food in advance. Makes 12, 6-inch pancakes.

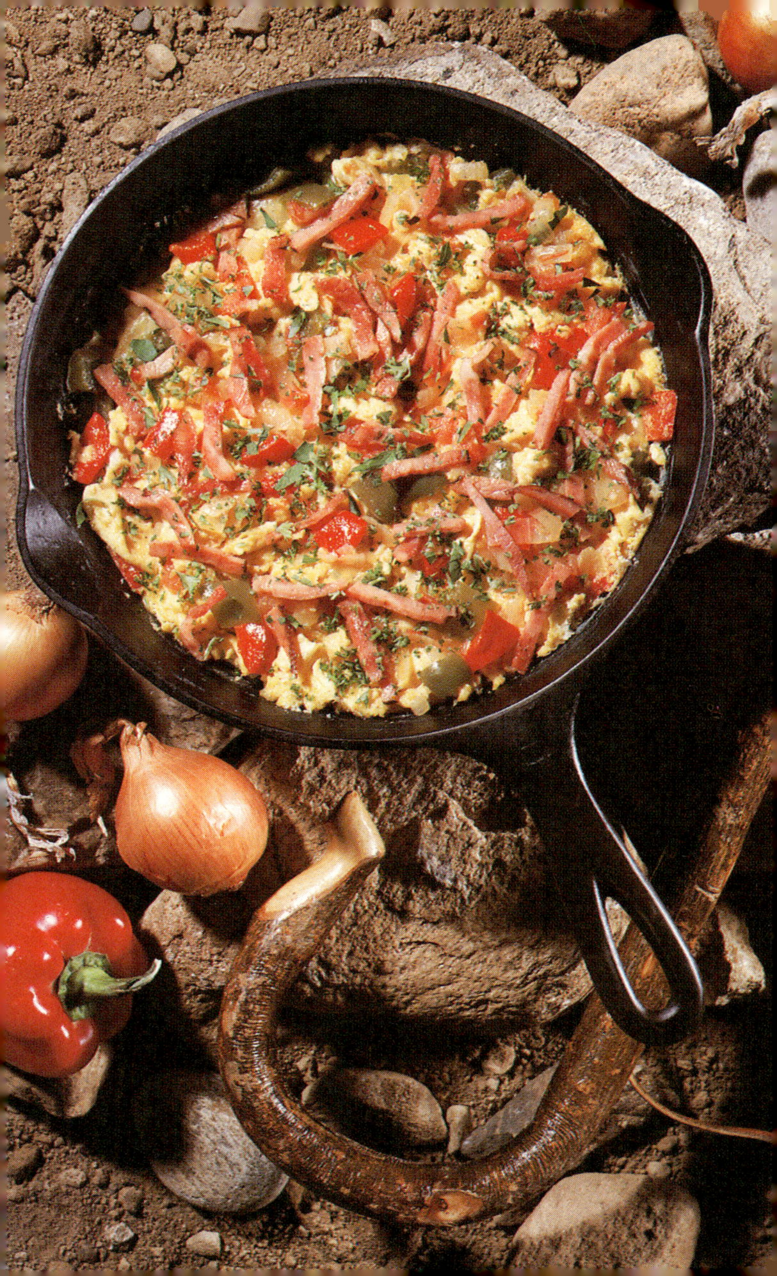

Cheese Pizza

Pizza Dough
- 8 ounces self-rising flour
- ½ level teaspoon salt
- 4 tablespoons margarine
- ½ cup milk

Topping
- 1 tablespoon oil
- 2 onions, chopped
- 1 (1-pound) can tomatoes, drained and chopped
- ½ pound cheese, thinly sliced
- 4 strips bacon, cut in half lengthwise

Make the pizza dough. Sift flour and salt into a large mixing bowl; add margarine, and rub it in with your fingertips. Stir in milk to make a soft dough. Put it onto a lightly floured board and knead gently. Roll out to a 12-inch diameter circle and place on a baking tray.

Make the topping: Heat oil in a large frying pan and fry onions until soft (about 5 minutes). Stir in tomatoes and cook for a further 2 minutes. Spread topping over pizza dough; cover with cheese slices and bacon strips. Bake in a 400°F oven for 20 to 25 minutes or until cooked. Serve immediately, or remove pizza from baking tray and leave to cool on a wire rack. Makes 6 servings.

Sandwiches

Austrian Panel Sandwich

1	(8-ounce) package cream cheese, softened
½	cup mayonnase
¼	teaspoon onion salt
¼	teaspoon celery salt
9	large thin slices dark pumpernickel bread
6	slices salami
6	slices mortadella

Place cream cheese in a small mixing bowl and beat with an electric mixer until smooth and fluffy. Add mayonnaise, onion salt, and celery salt, then mix until well combined.

Spread cream cheese mixture over all the slices of bread, then stack 3 slices together to make 3 sandwiches. Fold 2 slices of salami and 2 slices of mortadella in half for each sandwich, then arrange on top of sandwiches. Makes 3 large sandwiches.

Avocado Sandwich

- ½ cup soft butter
- 1 tablespoon basil, crumbled
- 6 slices cornbread
- 6 slices bacon
- 1 ripe avocado, sliced
- 12 cherry tomatoes, halved
- 12 canned pitted California ripe olives
- Salt and pepper to taste
- 1 lime

Combine butter and basil and blend well, then spread over the cornbread Cut bacon slices in half and fry until crisp. Arrange bacon strips, avocado slices, tomato halves, and ripe olives on cornbread; sprinkle with salt and pepper.

Cut lime into 6 wedges and garnish each sandwich with a wedge. Lime juice may be squeezed over sandwiches. Makes 6 open-faced sandwiches.

Barbecued Bologna Sandwiches

- 1 pound chunk of bologna, unsliced
- 6 Kaiser rolls
- ¾ cup pears or pineapple, chopped
- 2 tablespoons canned relish
- ¼ teaspoon dried mustard (powder)
- Potato chips (optional)

Slice bologna into 6 thick slices. Grill them on the barbeque grill for 5 to 10 minutes each side, or until nicely grilled and sizzling. Serve each on a Kaiser roll, topped with mixture of pears, relish, and mustard. Serve with potato chips. Makes 6 sandwiches.

Grilled Cheese-Peanut Butter Sandwich

- 16 slices enriched bread
- 4 tablespoons soft butter or margarine
- ½ cup peanut butter
- ½ cup (4 ounces) pimiento cream cheese
- 4 slices American cheese

Spread all the bread with butter or margarine; then spread 4 slices with pimiento cream cheese, using 2 tablespoons on each slice. Cover with the second slice of bread. Spread this slice with peanut butter, using 2 tablespoons on each; cover with a third slice of bread. Place 1 slice American cheese on this layer, and top with the fourth slice of bread.

Cut sandwiches into thirds. Insert a toothpick into each cut section; place cut-side down on a cookie sheet. Toast under a preheated broiler 5 minutes on each side. Serve with fruit salad. Makes 4 servings.

Eggs on Potato Cakes

Bologna Salad Sandwich Filling

½ cup (3 ounces) ground bologna sausage	1 tablespoon onion, chopped
1 hard-cooked egg, chopped	2 tablespoons mayonnaise or salad dressing
2 tablespoons sweet pickles, chopped	¼ teaspoon salt

Combine bologna sausage, chopped egg, sweet pickle, onion, mayonnaise, and salt. Makes filling for 4 sandwiches.

"Stack" Bunwiches

8 large round soft buns	2 pounds assorted sliced ready-to-serve meats (bologna, liver sausage, spiced ham, tongue, ham, salami, etc.)
½ cup prepared mustard	
1 cup pickle relish	

Split buns crosswise; spread bottom slices lightly with mustard. Pile alternate slices of 3 or 4 different kinds of ready-to-serve meats on bottom slice of each bun, then spread slices with relish and mustard. Place bun tops on sandwiches. Makes 8 servings.

Cheese and Ham Dreams

8 slices bread	Prepared mustard
Butter	4 slices ham
4 slices cheese	

Butter bread on 1 side. Place a slice of cheese on 4 of the slices of bread; spread with a little mustard. The buttered side of the bread will be for grilling. Cover with ham and make 4 sandwiches by placing remaining slices of buttered bread on top, buttered-side out.

Toast sandwiches in a frying pan or under a hot grill until golden on both sides. Makes 4 servings.

Cheeseburgers

1½ cups (½ pound) grated processed or American cheese	½ teaspoon Worcestershire sauce
2 tablespoons onion, finely chopped	¼ teaspoon salt
⅓ cup sweet pickles, chopped	½ cup mayonnaise or salad dressing
2 hard-cooked eggs, chopped	6 hamburger buns

Combine cheese, onion, pickles, eggs, Worcestershire, salt, and mayonnaise. Cut buns in half; spread 1/4 cup cheese mixture on bottom half of each bun. Place all halves of the buns, cut-side up, on a cookie sheet; toast under a preheated broiler 5 minutes, or until the tops are toasted and cheese melts. Makes 6 servings.

Filled Pancakes

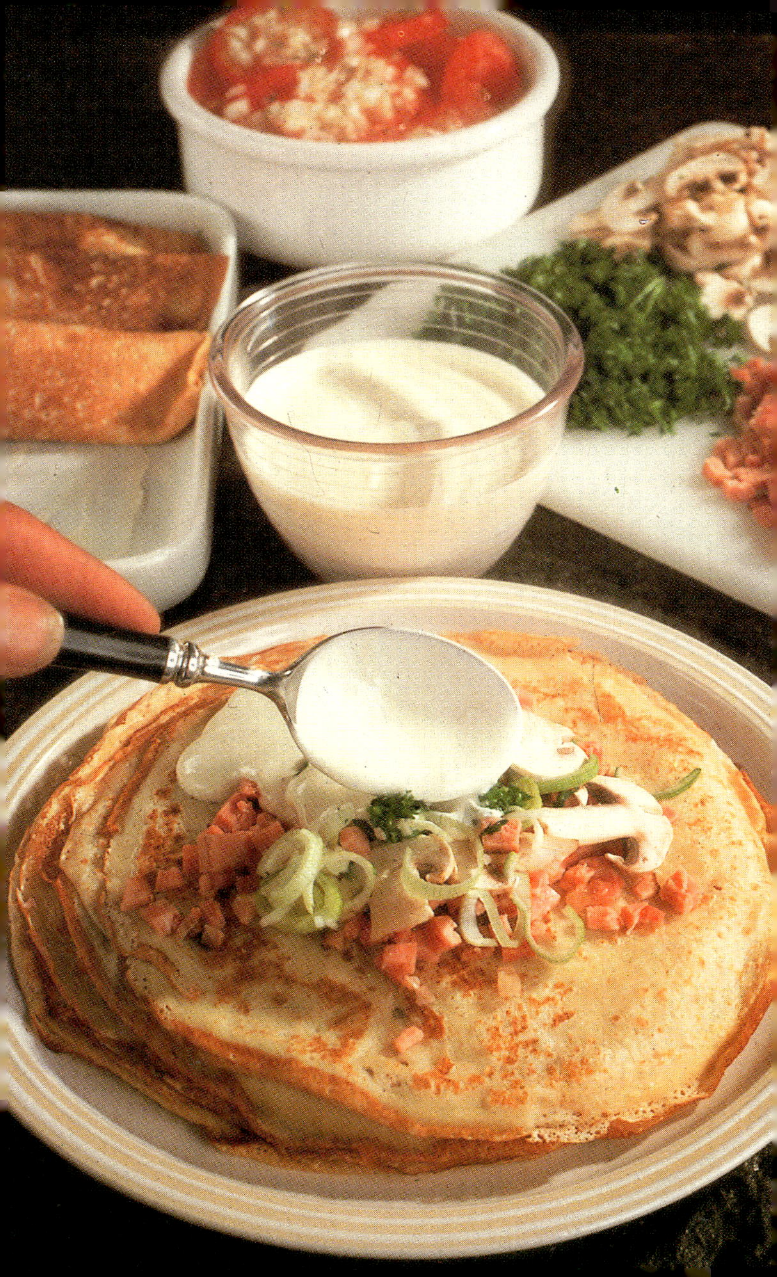

Chickenburgers

1	pound twice-ground raw chicken meat	¼	cup enriched bread crumbs
1	teaspoon salt	2	tablespoons milk
⅛	teaspoon pepper	1	tablespoon parsley, minced
1	egg		

Combine ingredients in order given. Mix thoroughly until smooth. Form into 8 round flat cakes a scant 1/2 inch thick. Slow-fry 12 minutes in butter or margarine. Serve on rolls. Makes 8 servings.

Open-Faced Chicken-Salad Sandwiches

- 4 slices toast
- ½ head Bibb lettuce, thinly sliced
- 8 to 12 ounces cooked chicken-breast meat, thinly sliced

Dressing
- ⅓ cup plain yogurt (can be part mayonnaise)
- 1 teaspoon horseradish
- 1 tablespoon catsup
- 2 tablespoons orange juice
- 1 tablespoon brandy
- Salt and pepper to taste

Topping
- 2 hard-cooked eggs, sliced or cut into wedges
- 2 medium tomatoes, sliced
- 8 canned pineapple chunks
- 2 maraschino cherries, halved

Top toast slices with lettuce. Arrange chicken on top.

Combine dressing ingredients; pour over chicken. Garnish each sandwich with egg, tomato, pineapple, and half a cherry. Serve at once. Makes 4 servings.

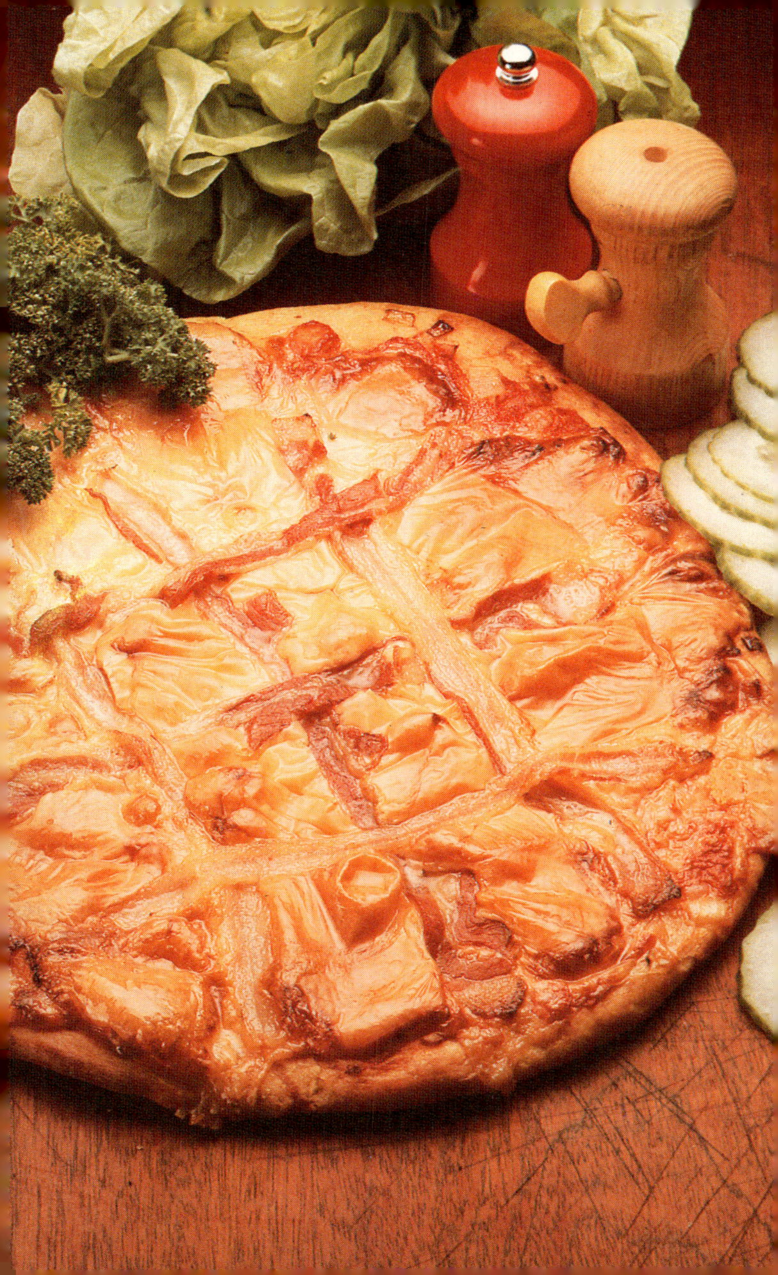

Club Sandwich

3 slices toast	2 slices cooked white
Butter or margarine	chicken meat
Lettuce	2 crisp cooked bacon slices
Mayonnaise	2 slices tomato

Toast bread and spread with butter or margarine. Cover 1 slice with chicken; spread with mayonnaise and top with a lettuce leaf. Cover with a slice of toast and spread with mayonnaise. Place bacon and tomato slices on top. Cover with remaining toast slice. Fasten securely with 4 wooden toothpicks.

Cut sandwich diagonally into 4 triangles. Stand them upright on a plate. Garnish with pickles, olives, or halved slices of tomato. Makes 1 serving.

Sautéed Soft Crab Sandwich

1 soft-shelled crab	Lettuce
Butter	Tomato
Red and black pepper	Mayonnaise
Rye or pumpernickel bread	Lemon juice or red hot sauce

In a skillet slightly larger than the crab, melt enough butter to coat pan liberally. When butter bubbles, gently lower crab into it with a spatula. Sprinkle on red or black pepper to taste. Sauté 2 to 3 minutes. Flip crab over; season with more pepper and continue cooking until top shell turns a deep red. Remove from heat.

Serve immediately on rye or soft pumpernickel bread, with lettuce, tomato, mayonnaise, lemon juice and/or red hot sauce. Makes 1 serving.

Cream Cheese-Raisin Sandwich Filling

½ cup seedless raisins	1 (3-ounce) package cream
½ cup water	cheese
	4 teaspoons milk

Soak raisins in water for 30 minutes. Pour liquid off. Combine cream cheese and milk until soft. Add raisins and mix well. Makes filling for 4 sandwiches.

Barbecued Bologna Sandwiches

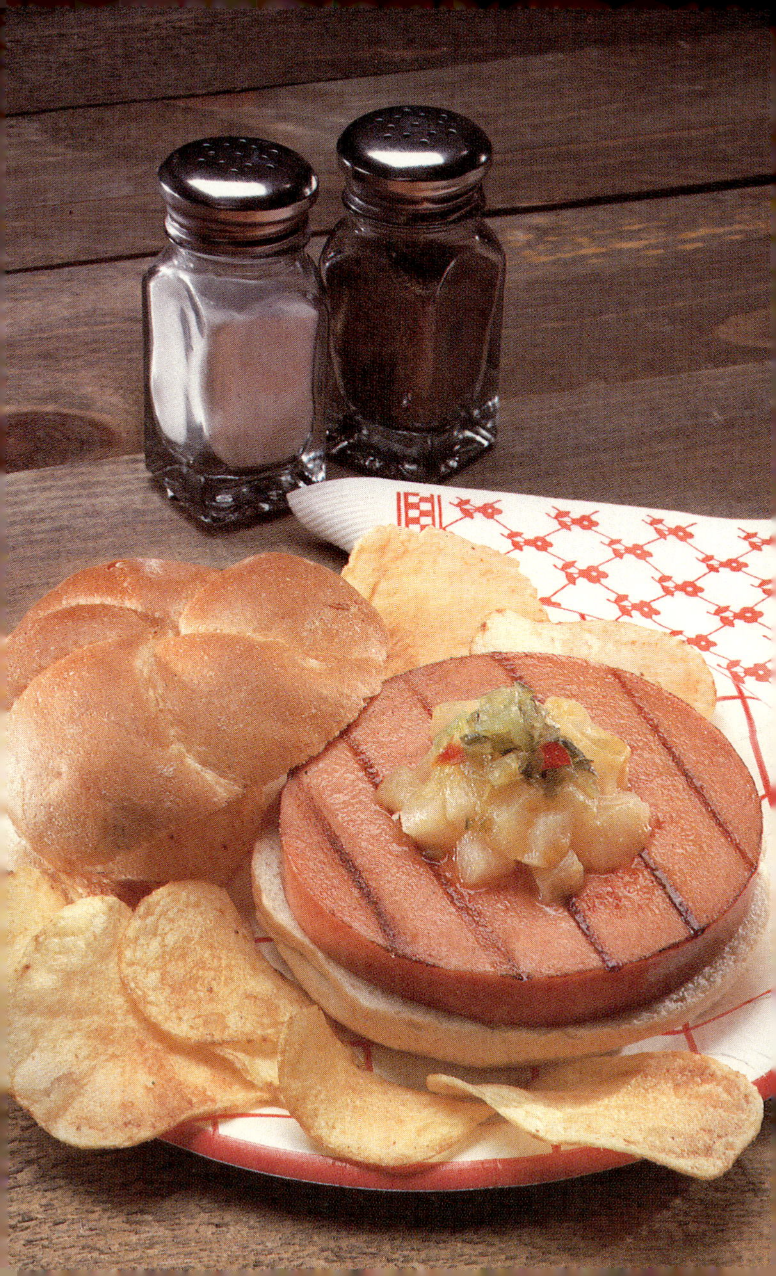

Corned Beef on Croissant

12 ounces cooked corned beef, thinly sliced	2 ounces Brie cheese, cut into thin slices
2 tablespoons butter, softened	4 large croissants, split
2 tablespoons Dijon-style mustard	

Thoroughly combine butter and mustard. To assemble sandwiches, spread cut side of each croissant with an equal amount of butter mixture. Place an equal amount of cheese on bottom half of each croissant. Arrange an equal portion of sliced corned beef over cheese. Close sandwiches with croissant top.

Wrap each sandwich securely in foil, making double folds to seal. Place packets in 350°F oven 10 to 15 minutes, or just until cheese melts. Makes 4 servings.

Fried Egg and Cheese Sandwich

8 slices bread	2 eggs, beaten
Butter	Salt and pepper
¼ pound cheese, grated	Oil for frying

Make sandwiches with bread, butter, and cheese. Beat eggs well and season. Dip sandwiches into egg. Heat oil in a frying pan and fry sandwiches quickly until golden. Drain on paper towels and serve very hot. Makes 4 servings.

Cucumber Sandwich

2 cucumbers	***Sour Cream Whip***
1½ teaspoons salt	¾ cup sour cream
6 slices whole wheat bread	1 teaspoon lemon juice
6 tablespoons soft butter	1 tablespoon green onions, thinly sliced
3 hard-boiled eggs, sieved	½ teaspoon salt
12 canned pitted California ripe olives, halved	
Sliced green onions	

Cheese and Ham Dreams

Peel cucumbers, then cut in very thin slices and sprinkle with salt. Chill for at least 30 minutes; squeeze out excess moisture. Spread bread with butter; then arrange cucumbers, sieved eggs, and olives on the bread.

Combine ingredients for sour cream whip and mix well. Top sandwiches with sour cream whip. and sprinkle with green onions. Cut into quarters to serve. Makes 6 open-faced sandwiches.

Spicy Eggplant Sandwiches

- 1 medium eggplant, about 1 pound
- 4 small French bread rolls
- ¼ cup Italian-style salad dressing
- 1 tomato, sliced into 4 slices
- 3 tablespoons olive oil
- ½ pound fresh mushrooms, sliced
- 1½ cups onion, thinly sliced
- 1 teaspoon oregano
- ¼ teaspoon salt
- ¼ teaspoon pepper
- 1 (6-ounce) package provolone cheese, sliced

Remove ends from eggplant; slice lengthwise into 4, 1/2-inch slices. Salt slices on both sides. Drain on paper towels 30 minutes.

Slice each bread roll in half horizontally; brush cut sides with salad dressing. Preheat broiler.

Heat 2 tablespoons of the oil in large skillet until very hot. Add drained eggplant; cook until nicely browned, about 8 minutes per side. Put 1 slice on bottom half of each roll. Cut each tomato slice in half and arrange 2 halves, slightly overlapping, over each eggplant slice.

Heat remaining 1 tablespoon oil in same skillet. Add mushrooms and cook until slightly brown and all their water has evaporated, about 5 minutes. Add onions, oregano, salt, pepper, and more oil if necessary. Cook until onions are slightly browned but still crisp-tender.

Divide onion mixture evenly among sandwiches, spreading over tomato slices. Top each sandwich with 2 overlapping cheese slices.

Put sandwiches on a cookie sheet. Broil, 8 inches from heat source, until cheese melts, about 3 to 5 minutes. Top with other half of roll and serve. Makes 4 servings.

Peanutty Egg Salad Sandwiches

- 3 tablespoons mayonnaise
- ⅛ teaspoon salt
- 4 hard-boiled eggs, chopped
- ¼ cup carrot, shredded
- ¼ cup celery, chopped
- ⅓ cup peanut butter, crunchy if preferred
- 8 slices bread, toasted

In medium bowl, blend together mayonnaise and salt. Stir in eggs, carrot, and celery. Spread 1 heaping tablespoon of peanut butter on each of 4 bread slices. Spread each with about 1/4 cup egg salad mixture. Top with remaining bread slices. Makes 4 servings.

Denver or Western Sandwich

- 1 teaspoon butter or margarine
- 1 egg
- 1 tablespoon onion, finely chopped
- 1 tablespoon green pepper, finely chopped
- 2 tablespoons milk
- ⅛ teaspoon salt
- 2 tablespoons cooked ham or crisp bacon, chopped
- Pinch of pepper
- 2 slices buttered rounds bread or toast

In a small skillet, heat butter until moderately hot. Meanwhile, beat the egg and add onion, green pepper, milk, ham, or bacon, salt, and pepper. Pour into skillet. Cook, stirring and lifting mixture to cook evenly.

At the same time, draw mixture toward center to keep it round and make a "cake" to fit the bread. Brown slightly on the bottom. Turn to cook other side. Place between bread or toast slices. Serve hot. Makes 1 serving.

Open-Faced Chicken-Salad Sandwiches

Fried Egg and Cheese Sandwich

Tasty Frankfurter Sandwich Filling

- ¾ cup (¼ pound) processed American cheese, grated
- 3 tablespoons milk
- 3 frankfurters, chopped
- 1 tablespoon prepared mustard

Combine cheese and milk in top of a double boiler; when cheese has melted, add chopped frankfurters and mustard; mix well. Makes approximately 1 cup, or filling for 5 sandwiches.

Hot Dogs

4 **frankfurters**	4 **hot dog rolls**
1 **tablespoon oil**	**French mustard (optional)**
2 **onions, sliced**	

Cook frankfurters in a saucepan of boiling water until piping hot. Heat oil in a frying pan and fry onion slices until soft and lightly browned. Cut rolls in half lengthwise; place 1 frankfurter in each roll with some onion rings and a little mustard if liked. Serve piping hot. Makes 4 servings.

Frankfurters with Fruit Sauce

1 **pound frankfurters**	4 **tablespoons vinegar**
1 **can apricots, about 1 cup**	**Salt and pepper**
1 **tablespoon Worcestershire sauce**	**Hot dog rolls for serving**
2 **level tablespoons soft brown sugar**	

Separate frankfurters. Drain apricots, but reserve the syrup. Press fruit through a sieve or puree in a food processor or electric blender. Add Worcestershire sauce, sugar, vinegar, and salt and pepper to the apricots, with enough of the syrup to make a thick pouring sauce. Heat gently, stirring until simmering.

Cook frankfurters over a hot fire, basting with sauce. Turn and baste frequently until hot (about 5 minutes). Put each frankfurter in a roll. Heat remaining sauce and spoon over frankfurters before serving. Makes 4 to 6 servings.

Savory French Toast Sandwiches

12 slices enriched or whole wheat bread	¾ cup milk
Butter or margarine, softened	¼ teaspoon salt
Cooked ham, chicken, turkey, or Swiss cheese, thinly sliced	⅛ teaspoon ground cinnamon, clove, or nutmeg
3 eggs	3 tablespoons butter or margarine

Lightly spread bread slices with softened butter or margarine. Put on ham, chicken, turkey, or cheese; put bread slices together in pairs. Cut in half if you like.

Beat eggs with the milk until frothy. Add salt and cinnamon, clove, or nutmeg. Dip sandwiches quickly in and out of egg mixture; fry in butter or margarine 4 minutes or until golden brown on both sides. Makes 6 sandwiches.

Greek Meat Pockets

¼ cup oil	Salt and pepper to taste
1 onion, finely chopped	3 cups leftover meat (beef, lamb, or pork), thinly sliced
1 clove garlic, chopped	8 Mid-East pocket breads
1 small eggplant, peeled and cut into 1-inch cubes	½ cup feta or farmer cheese, finely crumbled
1 large tomato, chopped	
1 cup tomato juice	
¼ teaspoon oregano, crumbled	

Heat oil in skillet; sauté onion and garlic 5 minutes. Add eggplant and tomato; stir over high heat until tomatoes are mushy. Stir in tomato juice and oregano. Add salt and pepper; cover. Simmer 15 to 20 minutes, until eggplant is tender and mixture thick.

Add meat; stir over low heat until hot and bubbly. Heat in 400°F oven 5 minutes, if desired. Cut 1/4-inch piece from top of each pocket; open. Fill with hot mixture; sprinkle with crumbled cheese. Makes 8 servings.

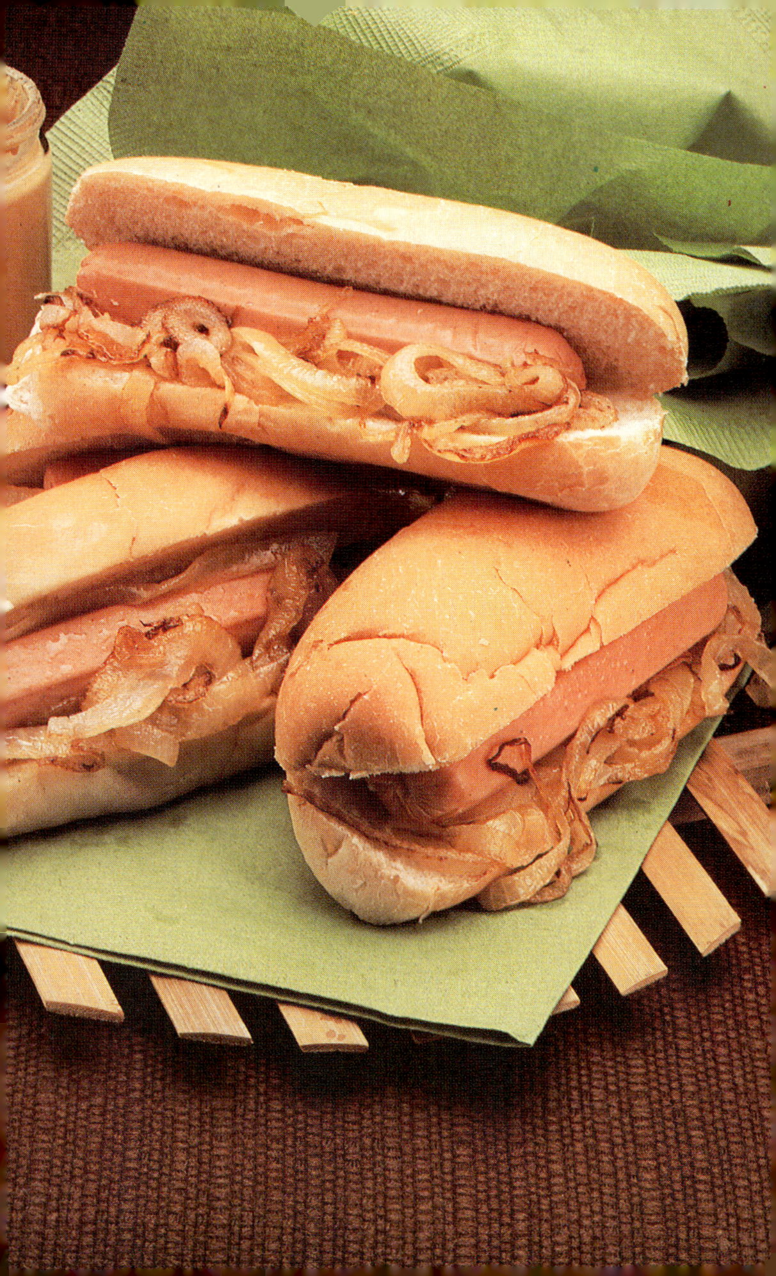

Ham Sandwich Loaf

1 loaf uncut bread	Mayonnaise
½ pound cooked ham, chopped	1 cup sweet pickle
1 can (about 3½ ounces) pimientos, drained and chopped	2 hard-boiled eggs
	Butter
	1 to 1½ cups cream cheese

Remove all crusts from bread and cut bread lengthwise into 4 equally thick slices.

Combine ham and pimientos; add enough mayonnaise to make spreadable paste.

Chop pickle and eggs together; moisten with mayonnaise.

Spread 1 slice of bread with butter, then with 1/2 the ham mixture. Butter both sides of second slice of bread; press over first slice. Spread with egg mixture. Butter both sides of third slice of bread; press on top of egg mixture; spread with remaining ham mixture. Butter bottom of top slice; press into position.

Place reshaped loaf onto serving platter; spread top and sides with thick layer of cream cheese. If this does not spread easily, soften with a little cream or milk. Refrigerate 3 to 4 hours; cut through in slices. Makes 7 or 8 servings.

Hamburgers

¼ cup stale bread	1 egg
1 pound ground beef	Oil for frying
1 small onion, grated	6 to 8 soft white rolls
Salt and pepper	Parsley for garnish
½ level teaspoon mixed dried herbs	

Remove crusts from bread; put bread into a bowl and cover with water. Leave for 2 to 3 minutes, then squeeze out as much of the water as possible. Put ground beef in a bowl, add the soaked bread, onion, salt and pepper, herbs, and egg. Beat all ingredients together thoroughly.

With wet hands, shape mixture into 6 or 8 patties. Heat a little oil in a frying pan and cook hamburgers for 2 to 3 minutes on each side. Serve in soft white rolls. Garnish with parsley. Makes 4 to 6 servings.

Frankfurters with Fruit Sauce

Giant Hero Sandwich

1 (3-ounce) package cream cheese, softened	Liver sausage slices
Mayonnaise	Swiss cheese slices
1 long loaf French bread	Fresh tomato wedges
Prepared mustard	Green and ripe olives
Ham slices	Small pickled onions
Salami slices	Gherkins
Sliced cooked pork	Endive
Bologna slices	Watercress

Place cream cheese in a small bowl, then stir in enough mayonnaise to make a smooth mixture of spreadable consistency. Cut bread in half lengthwise. Spread each half with cheese mixture, then mustard. Arrange remaining ingredients on bottom half of the bread. Place top half over filling, then cut diagonally into 6 pieces to serve. Makes 6 servings.

Lamb Burgers in Pita Pockets

¼ cup bulgur wheat	¼ teaspoon salt
Warm water	¼ teaspoon pepper
1 pound ground lamb	2 whole wheat pita breads with pockets
1 tablespoon dry red wine	Lettuce leaves
1 tablespoon parsley, finely chopped	
1 clove garlic, minced	
½ teaspoon fresh mint, minced	

Cover bulgur in warm water and soak 1 hour. Drain well.

Mix drained bulgur, lamb, wine, parsley, garlic, mint, salt and pepper in large bowl. Shape mixture into four patties.

Grill patties about 8 inches from hot coals, turning once, until desired degree of doneness, about 10 minutes total for medium-rare.

Cut pita bread crosswise in half. Fill pocket with lettuce leaves. Top with lamb. Serve immediately. Makes 4 servings.

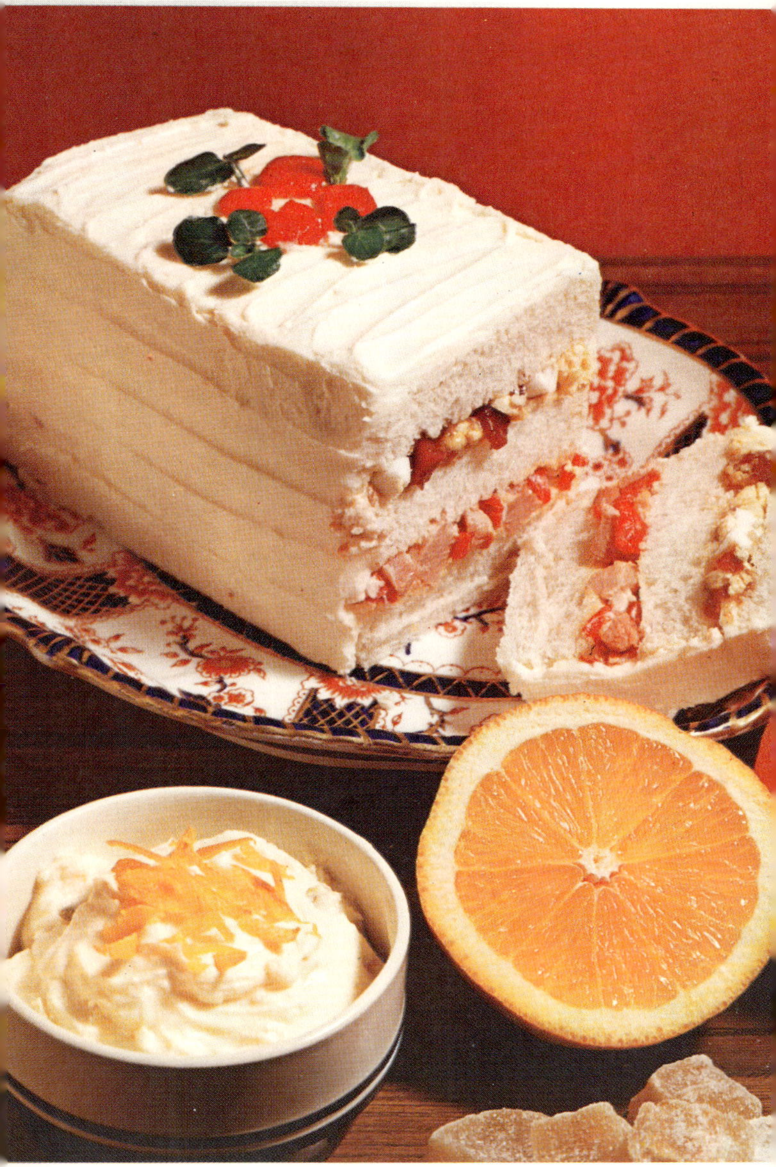

Long Sandwich with Salami

1 loaf Italian bread, sliced in half lengthwise	1 cup half-and-half
12 salami slices	½ cup white wine
Butter	White pepper to taste
¼ pound fresh mushrooms, sliced	Celery salt to taste
	3 tomatoes, skinned
¼ cup all-purpose flour	4 to 6 slices mozzarella cheese

Place bread, cut-side-up, on a jelly-roll pan. Bake in preheated 425°F oven until golden. Remove pan from oven and keep oven hot.

Arrange salami slices on toasted bread. Melt 1/4 cup of butter in a heavy saucepan. Add mushrooms and sauté until golden. Remove mushrooms with a slotted spoon and arrange over salami.

Add enough butter to the remaining butter in saucepan to measure 1/4 cup, then place over low heat to melt. Stir in flour to make a smooth paste. Add cream, stirring constantly, then cook until thickened. Stir in wine and seasonings, then cook, stirring, until sauce is very thick and the flavors blended.

Cut tomatoes into thin slices. Spread sauce over mushrooms and salami, then arrange tomatoes over sauce so that slices overlap slightly. Place cheese slices over top of sandwich, covering as evenly as possible. Bake until cheese is melted. Makes 4 servings.

Monte Cristo Sandwich

8 slices bread	4 slices cooked ham
2 eggs	4 slices Swiss cheese
½ cup milk	Prepared mustard
½ teaspoon salt	Butter for frying
Pinch of pepper	
Sliced breast of chicken or turkey	

Cut crusts from bread. Beat eggs, milk, salt, and pepper together; dip bread slices in mixture. Let soak well; drain. Arrange some thin slices of chicken on 4 bread slices. Cover with slice of ham; top with slice of cheese. Spread lightly with mustard; cover each with another slice of bread. Press down well; cut across diagonally.

Heat butter in skillet; fry sandwiches until brown and crisp; turning once. Serve hot. Makes 4 servings.

Sandwiches/79

Beefburgers

Stuffed Picnic Loaf

1	large unsliced sandwich loaf of bread
1	envelope unflavored gelatin
2	(7-ounce) cans chunk-style tuna, drained and flaked
¾	cup cooked potatoes, diced
¾	cup cooked green peas
¾	cup cooked green beans, chopped
¾	cup cooked carrots, diced
2	hard-boiled eggs, chopped
6	tablespoons half-and-half
½	teaspoon pepper, freshly ground
1	teaspoon salt
2	teaspoons paprika
1	cup mayonnaise

Slice crust from 1 end of sandwich loaf and reserve. Scoop out center of the loaf, leaving a 1/4-inch shell.

Soften gelatin in 1/4 cup of water, then dissolve over hot water. Combine tuna, potatoes, green peas, green beans, carrots, and eggs in a large bowl and blend well. Stir in cream, pepper, salt, paprika, mayonnaise, and gelatin and blend thoroughly.

Spoon tuna mixture into prepared shell and pack firmly. Cut off excess bread shell; if tuna mixture does not fill shell, then replace reserved crust. Wrap loaf tightly with aluminum foil and refrigerate until chilled. Cut into slices to serve. Makes 20 to 24 slices.

Chilled Pinwheels

1 loaf close-textured bread
Creamed butter, softened cheese, or any very smooth spread
Green pepper strips
Pimiento strips
About 4 stuffed olives (optional)
Soft butter

Remove crusts from top and sides of bread. With sharp knife, cut bread lengthwise in slices 1/8 to 1/4 inch thick; discard bottom crust. Spread long slices of bread with creamed butter. Lay alternating strips of green pepper and pimiento crosswise, 1 inch apart, over entire strip of bread; or lay olives lengthwise on one end of bread.

Beginning at one end, roll bread as for jelly roll. Spread a little soft butter on last lap of bread to make it stick; wrap rolls in waxed paper. Place in refrigerator to chill. When ready to serve, slice about 1/4 inch thick. Makes 6 servings.

Prosciutto under Cover

- 1 loaf Italian bread, sliced in half lengthwise
- 6 to 8 slices Port du Salut cheese or 1 (3-ounce) package cream cheese
- ¼ cup leek, minced
- 12 slices prosciutto or pastrami
- 1 tablespoon capers
- 2 large eggs, separated
- 1 cup mayonnaise

Place bread, cut-side-up, on a baking sheet. Bake in a preheated 425°F oven until golden. Arrange cheese slices on toasted bread, then sprinkle leek over cheese. Place prosciutto slices over cheese and sprinkle with capers.

Beat egg yolks slightly, then stir into mayonnaise, mixing well. Beat egg whites until stiff, but not dry. Fold 1/4 of egg whites into mayonnaise mixture thoroughly; then fold in remaining egg whites carefully. Spread mayonnaise mixture evenly over sandwich.

Bake in a preheated 400°F oven for 8 to 10 minutes or until topping is golden brown. Serve immediately. Makes 4 servings.

Giant Hero Sandwich

Skewered Pineapple-Salami Sandwiches

1 (16-ounce) can sliced pineapple	Dash of garlic powder
6 (3-inch thick) slices sourdough bread	12 slices mozzarella cheese
½ cup butter, softened	12 slices salami
½ teaspoon mixed Italian herbs	2 eggs
	½ cup milk
	¾ cup Parmesan cheese, freshly grated

Drain pineapple. Cut 2 slits, 1 inch apart, in each bread slice from top to bottom, leaving bottom crust intact. Mix butter, Italian herbs, and garlic powder, then spread on the cut sides of each slit. Trim mozzarella cheese slices to same size as salami slices. Place 1 cheese slice on each salami slice and roll as for jelly roll. Insert 1 pineapple slice in 1 slit and 2 salami-wrapped cheese slices in the other slit of each slice of bread. Secure each sandwich with 2 wooden picks.

Place eggs in a shallow bowl and beat well. Add milk and mix until combined, then dip sandwiches into egg mixture to lightly moisten surfaces. Place on a buttered baking sheet and sprinkle with Parmesan cheese. Bake in a preheated 400°F oven for about 15 minutes or until browned. Place in a serving dish and garnish with cherry tomatoes and parsley. Makes 6 servings.

Shrimp Sandwich

½ pound fresh shrimp	12 canned pitted California ripe olives
Dry sherry	2 tablespoons parsley, chopped
3 tablespoons lemon juice	Pepper to taste
4 slices light rye bread	
3 tablespoons soft butter	
4 ounces cream cheese	

Boil the shrimp for 5 minutes, stirring occasionally; remove from heat and cover. Let stand for 15 minutes. Drain in colander, then cool; peel and devein.

Add 3 tablespoons sherry and lemon juice to shrimp and toss until coated. Let stand for 30 minutes.

Spread bread with butter. Soften cream cheese to room temperature, then mix with 2 teaspoons sherry. Spread cream cheese mixture on the buttered bread. Drain shrimp and cut olives in half, then arrange over cream cheese. Sprinkle parsley and pepper over the top Cut into quarters. Makes 16 canapés.

Monte Cristo Sandwich

Hot Salmon and Cheese Rolls

1 small can salmon	4 hamburger rolls
1 package frozen peas	Butter
1 small can evaporated milk	4 slices American or processed cheese
Salt and pepper	
Lemon juice	

Drain and flake fish. Add peas and evaporated milk; season with salt, pepper, and lemon juice. Stir over low heat until mixture is smooth and creamy.

Split rolls; spread with butter. Put slice of cheese on half of each one. Pile some hot fish mixture on top; cover with other half of roll. Serve at once. Makes 4 servings.

Pizza Burgers

- 1½ pounds ground beef
- ½ cup onion, chopped
- ¾ teaspoon garlic salt
- ¼ teaspoon pepper

Sauce
- 2 cups Italian-style tomatoes, peeled and broken up with fork
- 1 (8-ounce) can tomato sauce
- ¼ cup canned mushrooms, chopped
- 1 teaspoon dried oregano, crumbled
- 6 large French rolls, split (or small individual French bread loaves)
- 8 ounces mozzarella cheese, sliced

Combine beef, onion, garlic salt, and pepper; form into 6 patties the size and shape of rolls.

Combine tomatoes, tomato sauce, mushrooms, and oregano in saucepan; heat. Broil burgers until done to taste; place on bottom half of rolls. Top with some sauce and cheese; garnish with additional tablespoon of sauce. Return to broiler until cheese melts. Serve open-face or topped with other half of roll. Makes 6 servings.

Sandwich Island

- 4 tablespoons lemon juice
- 8 flounder fillets, fresh or frozen (thawed)
- 6 tablespoons oil
- 1 teaspoon salt
- 3 tablespoons flour

Sauce
- 1 medium cucumber
- 1 bunch dill
- ½ cup cream
- 1 teaspoon mustard
- 1 teaspoon lemon juice
- Pinch of salt
- Pinch of sugar

Other Ingredients
- 8 slices white bread
- 3 tablespoons butter
- 8 pieces green lettuce
- ½ bunch parsley

Add lemon juice to fish fillets and let stand for 10 minutes.

Heat oil in a pan. Salt the fillets and dip them in flour. Fry fillets to a golden brown on each side (about 2 minutes) and set them aside to drain on paper towels.

To make the sauce, peel cucumber and dice it very fine. Chop dill very fine. Beat cream in a bowl until it is very stiff. Spice cream with mustard, lemon juice, salt, and sugar. Add cucumber and dill.

Stuffed Picnic Loaf

Remove crusts from bread and spread the bread with a thin layer of butter. Place fish fillets on bread and cover them thinly with sauce. Top each with another piece of bread, placing buttered side to the bottom. Cut bread in half. Set sandwich on a piece of lettuce and garnish it with parsley. Makes 8 servings.

Grilled Deep-Sea Sandwiches

1 (12-ounce) package frozen haddock or cod fillets, partly thawed	8 slices bread or 4 hot dog or hamburger rolls, split
½ cup water	Softened butter
½ teaspoon salt	
¼ cup light cream	*Cheese Sauce*
¼ cup catsup	1 tablespoon butter
2 tablespoons sweet pickle, chopped	1 tablespoon flour
1 tablespoon onion, grated	¼ teaspoon salt
2 teaspoons prepared horseradish	Dash of pepper
½ teaspoon salt	¾ cup light cream or milk
Dash of pepper	¾ cup grated sharp Cheddar cheese or 1 cup mild Cheddar or process cheese

Cut fish into 1-inch pieces. Place fish, water, and 1/2 teaspoon salt in a saucepan. Cover, bring to a boil, and simmer until fish is easily flaked with a fork, about 5 minutes. Drain and flake the fish.

Combine cream, catsup, pickle, onion, horseradish, salt, and pepper. Add flaked fish and mix well. Spread on bread, making 4 sandwiches. Spread outside of sandwiches with softened butter. Brown in sandwich grill or sauté in a skillet. Serve with cheese sauce or top with a slice of cheese.

To make cheese sauce, melt butter in saucepan. Add flour, salt, and pepper and stir until blended. Then add cream gradually, stirring constantly. Cook and stir over medium heat until smooth and thickened. Add cheese and stir until melted. Makes 4 servings.

Sardine, Ham, and Bacon Sandwich

12 sardines	1 teaspoon lemon juice
1 cup cooked ham, chopped	12 slices bread or toast
2 tablespoons sweet pickles, chopped	2 tablespoons lettuce, shredded
1 teaspoon prepared mustard	1 tablespoon mayonnaise
1 teaspoon catsup	12 slices broiled bacon

Remove skin and bones from sardines; chop with ham and pickles. Add mustard, catsup, and lemon juice; mix well. Spread on 6 slices buttered bread. Sprinkle with lettuce; dot with mayonnaise.

Arrange 2 slices bacon on each sandwich; top with another slice buttered bread. Makes 6 servings.

Skewered Pineapple-Salami Sandwiches

Spanish Sandwiches

- 2 tablespoons pimiento, chopped
- 2 tablespoons onion, chopped
- 1 tablespoon butter
- 1 cup tomato juice
- 1 cup cheese, grated
- ½ teaspoon salt
- Dash of paprika
- 1 egg, well beaten
- 4 slices buttered toast

Sauté pimiento and onion in butter 5 minutes. Add tomato juice, cheese, salt, and paprika; cook 5 minutes or until cheese is melted. Stir small amount into egg. Return to hot mixture; cook 2 minutes. Serve on hot toast. Makes 4 servings.

Steak and Cheese Sandwiches

- ½ cup cider vinegar
- ½ cup Italian salad dressing
- ¼ tablespoon soy sauce
- 1 clove garlic, minced
- 1 bay leaf
- ¼ teaspoon freshly ground pepper
- 1½ pounds flank steak
- 2 tablespoons oil
- 2 medium onions, sliced and separated into rings
- 2 medium green peppers, ends removed, seeded and cut into ½-inch strips
- 6 French-style rolls
- 6 slices provolone cheese

Mix vinegar, salad dressing, soy sauce, garlic, bay leaf, pepper, and oil in large bowl. Add steak; stir so meat is covered with marinade. Cover with plastic wrap and refrigerate overnight.

Heat oil over medium-high heat in large skillet; add onions and peppers and cook until just crisp-tender. Remove with slotted spoon to small bowl; set aside.

Heat oven to 200°F. Cut rolls lengthwise (halfway through), wrap in foil and put in oven until warmed through.

Remove steak from marinade and drain. Cut steak against grain into 1/4-inch thick strips. Add to skillet and cook, stirring until they reach desired doneness. Remove meat from skillet and divide evenly on bottom halves of rolls. Divide onion-pepper mixture evenly over meat; cover each with a slice of cheese.

Put into oven to melt cheese. Cover top with remaining half of roll and serve. The cut roll can be brushed with some of the pan juices, if desired. Makes 6 servings.

Toasted Supper Sandwich

- 1 egg
- 1 tablespoon milk
- 1 tablespoon margarine
- 2 ounces mushrooms, sliced
- 4 slices bacon
- 4 slices bread
- Butter for spreading
- Sprigs of watercress for garnish

Beat egg with milk in a small saucepan. Place over low heat and gently scramble egg, stirring occasionally. Heat margarine in a frying pan, add sliced mushrooms, and fry for 1 to 2 minutes. Drain.

Fry bacon slices until crisp and drain. Toast slices of bread and spread with butter. Place one piece of toast on a plate; arrange sautéed mushrooms on it. Top with a second piece of toast and layer that with the scrambled egg. Put on a third piece of toast, lay the bacon on that, and finish with the last piece of toast. Garnish with a sprig of watercress. Serve cut in half. Makes 2 servings.

Salmon and Cheese Rolls (hot)

Sunday Double-Decker Sandwich

8 slices white bread	4 large tomatoes, sliced
½ cup butter	1 cup onion, chopped
8 slices bacon, halved	8 slices American cheese (or 4 cups grated cheese)
2 teaspoons mustard (optional)	

Preheat broiler.

Remove bread crusts; toast bread on one side only. Spread untoasted side with butter; lay bacon slices on bread. Broil until bacon is cooked; spread with mustard. Place tomatoes on bacon. Brush with a little melted butter; broil a few minutes. Sprinkle onion over tomato; broil another minute. Cover with cheese. (If using grated cheese, make sure tomatoes are thickly covered.) Broil until cheese bubbles.

Pile one on top of another to make 4 sandwiches; broil again until top layer of cheese is well browned. Serve at once. Makes 4 servings.

Sunday Double-Decker Sandwich

Grilled Tomato-Burgers

- 1½ pounds ground beef
- 1 teaspoon salt
- ⅛ teaspoon pepper
- 4 firm, ripe tomatoes
- 1 sweet onion, sliced into rings
- 6 large mushroom caps, cooked or canned, marinated in Italian-style low-calorie salad dressing

Lightly mix meat with salt and pepper; shape into 6 burgers. Cook on outdoor grill, cook in skillet, or broil as desired.

Cut each tomato into 3 slices, crosswise. Lightly brown with hamburgers for a few minutes, being sure tomatoes remain firm. Place each hamburger on a tomato slice; top with another slice. Arrange a few onion rings on top and put a mushroom cap in center. Garnish serving platter with additional onion rings if desired. Makes 6 servings.

Herbed Tuna Sandwiches

6	small French bread rolls or hard rolls	1	(6-ounce) can pitted black olives, sliced
1	bunch curly lettuce leaves	6	tablespoons olive oil
1	(13-ounce) can white tuna in water, drained and flaked	2	tablespoons each, minced: fresh thyme, oregano and basil leaves
2	tomatoes sliced		
1	large red onion, sliced, rings separated		

Slice rolls horizontally in half. Arrange lettuce leaves on rolls. Top with tuna, tomato slices, onion slices, and olives.

Mix minced herbs in small bowl. Sprinkle each sandwich with 1 tablespoon olive oil and 1 tablespoon mixed herbs. Makes 6 servings.

Tuna Heroes

4	individual hero rolls, split	American cheese, cut in strips
Romaine lettuce		Pimiento-stuffed olives, sliced
1	(6½- to 7-ounce) can tuna, drained	¼ cup mayonnaise
2	tablespoons sweet pickle relish	2 tablespoons catsup

Cover bottom halves of hero rolls with romaine. Break tuna into pieces, toss with pickle relish, and spread over romaine. Top with strips of cheese and olive slices.

Mix mayonnaise and catsup together; spoon over all. Cover with top halves of hero rolls. Makes 4 servings.

Tuna Danish Slim Sandwich

2 (6½- or 7-ounce) cans water-packed tuna	1 tablespoon catsup
1 cup cabbage, coarsely grated	1 tablespoon lemon juice
⅔ cup carrot, coarsely grated	½ teaspoon salt
3 tablespoons low-calorie salad dressing (mayonnaise-type)	Dash of pepper
	6 lettuce leaves
	6 slices low-calorie bread, toasted
	18 cucumber slices

Drain tuna; flake. Combine cabbage, carrot, and tuna. Combine dressing, catsup, lemon juice, salt, and pepper. Add to tuna mixture; blend thoroughly.

Place lettuce on toast. Place approximately 1/3 cup tuna salad on each lettuce leaf. Arrange 3 cucumber slices diagonally across each sandwich. Makes 6 servings.

Surprise Burgers

4 round crispy rolls	Salt and pepper
2 tablespoons butter, melted	2 tomatoes, skinned and chopped
4 eggs	1 tablespoon parsley, chopped
1 tablespoon milk	
2 tablespoons butter	

Slice a small round off the top of the rolls and scoop out some of the inside crumb. Brush inside of rolls with melted butter and bake in a 350°F oven for 5 minutes.

Combine eggs, milk, salt, and pepper. Melt butter and stir in eggs. Cook gently, stirring all the time, until eggs become soft and creamy. Stir in tomato and parsley. Pile into the hot rolls, replace the lids, and serve hot. Makes 4 servings.

Sandwiches/93

Surprise Burgers

EQUIVALENT MEASURES

dash = 2 or 3 drops
pinch = amount that can be held between ends of thumb & forefinger

1 tablespoon = 3 teaspoons
¼ cup = 4 tablespoons
⅓ cup = 5 tablespoons + 1 teaspoon
½ cup = 8 tablespoons
1 cup = 16 tablespoons
1 pint = 2 cups
1 quart = 4 cups
1 gallon = 4 quarts
1 peck = 8 quarts
1 bushel = 4 pecks
1 pound = 16 ounces

KITCHEN METRIC

measurements you will encounter most often in recipes are: centimeter (cm), milliliter (ml), gram (g), kilogram (kg)

cup equivalents (volume):

¼ cup = 60 ml
⅓ cup = 85 ml
½ cup = 125 ml
⅔ cup = 170 ml
¾ cup = 180 ml
1 cup = 250 ml
1¼ cups = 310 ml
1½ cups = 375 ml
2 cups = 500 ml
3 cups = 750 ml
5 cups = 1250 ml

spoonful equivalents (volume):

⅛ teaspoon = .5 ml
⅓ teaspoon = 1.5 ml
½ teaspoon = 3 ml
¾ teaspoon = 4 ml
1 teaspoon = 5 ml
1 tablespoon = 15 ml
2 tablespoons = 30 ml
3 tablespoons = 45 ml

pan sizes (linear & volume):

1 inch = 2.5 cm
8-inch square = 20-cm square
9 × 13 × 1½-inch = 20 × 33 × 4-cm
10 × 6 × 2-inch = 25 × 15 × 5-cm
13 × 9 × 2-inch = 33 × 23 × 5-cm
7½ × 12 × 1½-inch = 18 × 30 × 4-cm
(above are baking dishes, pans)
9 × 5 × 3-inch = 23 × 13 × 8-cm
(loaf pan)
10-inch = 25 cm   12-inch = 30-cm
(skillets)
1-quart = 1-liter   2-quart = 2-liter
(baking dishes, by volume)
5- to 6-cup = 1.5-liter
(ring mold)

weight (meat amounts; can & package sizes):

1 ounce = 28 g
½ pound = 225 g
¾ pound = 340 g
1 pound = 450 g
1½ pounds = 675 g
2 pounds = 900 g
3 pounds = 1.4 kg (in recipes, amounts of meat above 2 pounds will generally be stated in kilograms)
10 ounces = 280 g
(most frozen vegetables)
10½ ounces = 294 g
(most condensed soups)
15 ounces = 425 g
(common can size)
16 ounces = 450 g
(common can size)
1 pound, 24 ounces = 850 g
(can size)

OVEN TEMPERATURES

275°F = 135°C
300°F = 149°C
325°F = 165°C
350°F = 175°C
375°F = 190°C
400°F = 205°C
425°F = 218°C
450°F = 230°C
500°F = 260°C

Note that Celsius temperatures are sometimes rounded off to the nearest reading ending in 0 or 5; the Celsius thermometer is the same as Centigrade, a term no longer used.

Index

Anchovy Sandwiches, 5
Appetizer Sandwiches, Grilled, 6
Austrian Panel Sandwich, 57
Avocado Sandwich, 58

Beef Tidbits, Gem, 53
Bologna
  Salad Sandwich Filling, 59
  Sandwiches, Barbecued, 58
Breads
  Apple, 38
  Apricot Nut, 40
  Banana, 39
  Cheddar Cheese, 41
  Date-Nut Loaf, 42
  Fruit Loaf, 43
  Hard Rye, Wafers, 44
  Walnut Brown, 46
Bugs on a Log, 6
Buns, French, 43
Butterscotch Brownies, 30

Caraway Biscuits with Ham Filling, 48
Cauliflower, Herb-Crusted, 6
Cheese
  Ball, 9
  Bread, Cheddar, 41
  Burgers, 60
  Cottage, Pie, Herb and, 50
  Cream, Raisin Sandwich Filling, 64
  -Croissant Bake, 47
  Fried, 8
  Grilled, Peanut Butter Sandwich, 58
  and Ham Dreams, 60
  and Herb Spread, 9
  Logs, California Walnut, 10
  Pie, 50
  Pizza, 56
  Potted Herb, 10
  Rounds, 12
  and Steak Sandwiches, 88
Chicken
  Burgers, 62
  Salad Sandwiches, Open-Faced, 62
Chips
  Garlic-Butter, 12
  Plantain, 11
  Tortilla, 12
Chocolate
  Balls, 30
  Covered Anything, 26
  -Delight Bars, 32
  -Wine Cookies, 32
Clam Savory, 14
Club Sandwich, 64
Cookies
  Chocolate Balls, 30
  Chocolate-Wine, 32
  Hussar's Kisses, 34
  Pretzel, 36
  Walnut Rum, 36
Corned Beef on Croissant, 66
Crab Sandwich, Sautéed Crab, 64
Cucumber Sandwich, 66

Dates, Blind, 26
Deep-Sea Sandwiches, Grilled, 86
Denver or Western Sandwich, 69
Doughnuts, Drop, 42

Egg(s)
  Basque Omelette, 52
  and Cheese Sandwich, Fried, 66
  Curry Spiced, 48
    on Potato Cakes, 53
  Salad Sandwiches, Peanutty, 68
  Spread, Favorite, 14
Eggplant Sandwiches, 68
Energy Pickups, Quick, 26

Frankfurter(s)
  with Fruit Sauce, 71
  Hot Dogs, 71
  Sandwich Filling, Tasty, 70
French Toast Sandwiches, Savory, 72

Garlic-Butter Chips, 12

Ham Sandwich Loaf, 74
Hamburgers, 74
Hartshorns, 34
Hero Sandwich, Giant, 76
Hot Dogs, 71
Hummus, 15

Jam Slices, 44

Lamb Burgers in Pita Pockets, 76
Long Sandwich with Salami, 78

Meat Pockets, Greek, 72
Melon
  à la Mode, 28
  Berry-Filled, 28
Monte Cristo Sandwich, 78
Mushrooms, Crumbed, 16

Omelette, Basque, 52
Olive Sandwich, 16
Orange Leek Sandwich, 15

Pancakes, Filled, 54
Party Mix, 16
Peanut Butter
  Grilled Cheese Sandwich, 58
  Ham Squares, 18
  Nuggets, 30
Pears in Chocolate Sauce, 28
Picnic Loaf, Stuffed, 80
Pineapple-Salami Sandwiches,
  Skewered, 82
Pinwheels, Chilled, 80
Pistachio
  Herbed, 19
  Puffs, 18
Pizza
  Burgers, 84
  Cheese, 56
Plantain Chips, 11
Popcorn, Cajun, 20
Pretzels
  Cookies, 36
  Sweet or Salty, 20
Prosciutto under Cover, 81

Quark Snacks, 22

Salami
  Long Sandwiches with, 78
  Sandwiches, Skewered Pineapple, 82
Salmon and Cheese Rolls, Hot, 83
Sandwich Island, 84
Sardine, Ham, and Bacon Sandwich, 86
Sausage
  and Apple Snacks, 22
  Links, Polish, 24
Shrimp Sandwich, 82
Spanish Sandwiches, 87
"Stack" Bunwiches, 60
Steak and Cheese Sandwiches, 88
Sunday Double-Decker Sandwich, 89
Surprise Burgers, 92

Toasted Supper Sandwich, 88
Tomato-Burgers, Grilled, 90
Tortilla Chips, 2
Tuna
  Danish Slim Sandwich, 92
  Heros, 91
  Sandwiches, Herbed, 91

Walnut Rum Cookies, 36
Western Sandwich, 69

Yogurt Cocktails, 25